MASTER THE A1 VOCABULARY IN JUST 21 DAYS

FRENCH SHORT STORIES

VOCABULARY
PERFECTION
SERIES

IN PARIS

BLACK SWAN LANGUAGES

Contents

Introduction

The Aims of This Book

"C'est en forgeant qu'on devient forgeron."

The French proverb above translates directly into the English as, "It is in forging that you become a blacksmith." In other words, it is only by actively practicing something new that one can eventually become proficient in that particular skill.

We've created this book with the aim of delighting learners in search of real French short stories for a more self-directed learning approach, as well as those with the more singular focus of mastering the complete A1 level vocabulary.

A Suggested 21-Day Schedule

Days 1 thru 8: For the first eight days, a fast-track schedule could comprise of reading two short story chapters each day. It would also be prudent to utilize the featured vocabulary lists to learn as many words and phrases as possible while reading the stories. This will help to save you some time when you are finished with the stories and ready to tackle the full glossary.

Days 9 thru 21: In the final thirteen days, a natural continuation of the fast-track schedule would focus on internalizing all of the vocabulary in the glossary following the short stories. Essentially, this glossary contains 830+ A1 level vocabulary based on resources focusing on the categories most likely to be tested by the official DELF (Diplôme d'Etudes en Langue Française, or Diploma in French studies) A1 level proficiency exam. (See the Resources chapter for links to these online resources.) A balanced workload distribution would suggest that each of the thirteen days should include internalizing at least 65 entries from the glossary. While many of the words will be familiar to those with previous French language study experience, it is also very doable for absolute beginners provided that ample time is set aside.

Important Disclaimers to Note

In the interest of an easier learning experience, a couple of "shortcuts" have been purposefully made within our glossary. They are as follows:

- **Masculine words and their feminine counterparts will be in the same line entry wherever possible.** Essentially, when the definite article (l') or the lack of a definite article precedes a masculine word line entry, there may be parentheses at the end of the French word containing additional letters such as (e), (ne), and the like, and these would effectively represent the feminine form of the word. For example, "l'Italien(ne)" would represent "l'Italien" (the Italian male person) together with "l'Italienne" (the Italian female person) as a compacted, single line entry in order to minimize the time and effort needed for the learner to internalize both of the gender forms.

- **The plural forms and parts of speech are largely omitted.** However, one can deduce the part of speech to a great extent by the parenthetical elements associated with each vocabulary word. Vocabulary which include (le), (la), (l') or (les) are always nouns, those which include (to) are always verbs, and those without parenthetical elements are adjectives, adverbs, prepositions, or something other than a noun or verb. Online French-English dictionaries are an invaluable resource to determine the oftentimes multiple parts of speech a particular word can encompass. Likewise, plural forms of French nouns can be easily found online via a search using terms like "plural of la fleur," where the final two words are respectively the gender-specific definite article and the singular French noun.

Don't agonize too much about the details of plural forms or parts of speech if this is your first time learning French vocabulary. Just remember to relax, focus, and enjoy the rewarding process of your language acquisition journey!

Get Ready to Experience the Magic of Paris in France!

The subsequent chapters will feature an extensive French alphabet and pronunciation guide, a fun primer to the French capital city of Paris, an original map pinpointing the story locations, the sixteen dual-language short stories, and a complete A1 vocabulary glossary. Are you ready to improve your French language skills? On y va ! (Let's go!)

The French Alphabet and How to Pronounce Almost Anything

The French Alphabet

This special chapter on the French alphabet and pronunciation of words in the French language is designed to allow learners across the entire spectrum, from absolute beginners to advanced speakers, to properly pronounce the words they encounter in French as well as internalize additional vocabulary words.

Each of the thirty-eight characters in the French alphabet below begins with a subheader showing how the letter is written (in quotation marks) and pronounced (in parentheses). These are all followed by three French words including the particular letter (in bold font), how they are pronounced (in phonetic marks), and the English translation (after the double forward slash).

Following this are thirteen subheader titles of some of the

most common letter combinations, demonstrating how the combination is written (in the first set of quotation marks) and then how the combination is phonetically pronounced (in the second set of quotation marks). These are followed by two French words including the particular letter combination (in bold font), how they are pronounced (in phonetic marks), and the English translation (after the double forward slash).

Take your time thoroughly reviewing this chapter and you will almost certainly be rewarded with an enormous boost in confidence in your French language reading abilities as well as a richer understanding of the core building blocks of this widely-spoken, global language!

The letter "A" (ah)...

Avignon (ah-vee-NYOHN) // Avignon

aimer (EE-meyh) // (to) like, (to) love

agréable (AH-gri-ah-bluh) // pleasant, nice, enjoyable

The letter "À" (A accent grave)...

voilà (VWHA-lah) // there is, there are, there you go

déjà (DEH-jah) // already

là-bas (LHA-bah) // over there

The letter "Â" (A accent circonflexe)...

âge (ahzh) // age

pâte (pahtt) // dough, paste

pâle (PAH-leh) // pale

The letter "B" (bey)...

Bordeaux (BHOHRH-dhoh) // Bordeaux

boire (bwhah) // (to) drink

bien (bhee-YHAN) // well, good

The letter "C" (sey)...

Cannes (kyannh) // Cannes

chercher (SHEHR-sheh) // (to) look for

charmant (SHAHRH-mhon) // charming

The letter "Ç" (C cédille)...

glaçon (GLAH-sohnh) // ice cube, block of ice, iceberg

français (FRAHN-seh) // French

çà et là (sah eyh lah) // here and there

The letter "D" (dey)...

Dijon (DEEH-jonh) // Dijon

danser (DONH-seyh) // (to) dance

difficile (DEEH-fhee-seelh) // difficult

The letter "E" (uhgh)...

Estonie (EHS-toh-nhee) // Estonia

enfourner (AHN-fohrh-neyh) // (to) put in the oven

entre (AHN-truh) // between

The letter "É" (E accent aigu)...

école (EEH-kohl-eh) // school

étudier (EYH-too-dee-eyh) // (to) study

élégant (EY-ley-ghonh) // elegant

The letter "È" (E accent grave)...

mère (MEH-yuh) // mother

père (PEH-yuh) // father

très (trheh) // very

The letter "Ê" (E accent circonflexe)...

fenêtre (FHOO-nhett) // window

être (EH-trh) // (to) be

même (mhemh) // same, even

The letter "Ë" (E tréma)...

Noël (NOH-ehlh) // Christmas

Citroën (SEEH-trhoh-ehn) // Citroën

ambiguë (AHN-bhee-gyooh) // ambiguous

The letter "F" (eff)...

France (fhrohnss) // France

finir (FHEE-neeh-uh) // (to) finish

fort (fhohrh) // strong

The letter "G" (zhey)...

Grenoble (GRUH-noh-bleh) // Grenoble

gagner (GAH-nyeyh) // (to) earn, (to) win, (to) gain

gentil (ZHAHN-teeh) // kind

The letter "H" (ahsh)...

Hermès (EYRH-mhes) // Hermès (French designer brand)

habiter (AH-beeh-teyh) // (to) live

hier (EEH-yeh-uh) // yesterday

The letter "I" (eeh)...

Irlande (EERH-lahn-dheh) // Ireland

imaginer (EEH-mah-jhee-neyh) // (to) imagine

ici (EEH-seeh) // here

The letter "Î" (I accent circonflexe)...

huître (oo-WEEHT) // oyster

boîte (bwhaht) // box, canister

traîneau (TRHEYH-nhoh) // sled, sleigh

The letter "Ï" (I tréma)...

maïs (MHAH-eehs) // corn

caraïbe (KYAH-rha-eeh-beh) // Caribbean

héroïque (EH-rhoh-eehkh) // heroic

The letter "J" (zheeh)...

Japon (JAH-pohnh) // Japan

jouer (jhoo-WHEY) // (to) play

jamais (JAH-meyh) // never

The letter "K" (kah)...

Kazakhstan (KAH-zhak-stohn) // Kazakhstan

klaxonner (KLAHK-soh-nhey) // (to) honk

kaki (KYAH-keeh) // khaki

The letter "L" (ell)...

Lyon (lee-YOHNH) // Lyon

lire (LEEH-yuh) // (to) read

léger (LHEE-zheyh) // lightz

The letter "M" (emm)...

Marseille (MAHRH-seyh) // Marseille

manger (MOHN-zheyh) // (to) eat

magnifique (MHAH-nhee-feekh) // magnificent

The letter "N" (en)...

Nice (neehs) // Nice

nager (NHA-zheyh) // (to) swim

noir (nwhah) // black

The letter "O" (oh)...

Oslo (OHS-loh) // Oslo

oublier (OO-blee-yeyh) // (to) forget

orange (OH-rahnzh) // orange

The letter "Ô" (O accent circonflexe)...

impôt (AHN-poh) // tax

tôt (toh) // early

chômant (SHOH-mahnh) // unemployed

The ligature "Œ" (e-dans-l'o)...

cœur (khehyuh) // heart

œuf (uhf) // egg

bœuf (bhuhf) // beef

The letter "P" (pey)...

Paris (PAH-rheeh) // Paris

parler (PAH-leyh) // (to) speak

petit (PUH-teeh) // small

The letter "Q" (koo)...

Qatar (KYAH-tahrh) // Qatar

quitter (KEE-teyh) // (to) leave

que (khuh) // that, than

The letter "R" (ehr)...

Reims (rhahns) // Reims

rire (RHEE-yuh) // (to) laugh

rien (rheeh-AHN) // nothing

The letter "S" (ess)...

Strasbourg (strhahs-BOOHRH) // Strasbourg

savoir (SAH-vwhah) // (to) know

sûr (SYOOH-uh) // on, sure, safe

The letter "T" (tey)...

Toulouse (TOOH-loohz) // Toulouse

travailler (TRHAH-vah-yhey) // (to) work

triste (trheehst) // sad

The letter "U" (oo)...

Ukraine (OO-khreyh-nuh) // Ukraine

utiliser (OO-tee-lee-zey) // (to) use

ultime (OOLH-teeh-mah) // ultimate, final, last

The letter "Û" (U accent circonflexe)...

mûre (MYOOH-uh) // blackberry

flûte (flyhooht) // flute

brûlé (BRHUY-leyh) // burnt

The letter "V" (vey)...

Versailles (VHEYRH-saih) // Versailles

vouloir (VOOH-lhwhah) // (to) want

vert (VEH-yuh) // green

The letter "W" (doo-blah-vey)...

Westminster (WHEYST-min-stuhrh) // Westminster

wagon (VAH-gohn) // railway car, wagon

week-end (WEEH-kehnh) // weekend

The letter "X" (eeks)...

Xertigny (ZEH-yah-tee-neeh) // Xertigny

xylophone (ZEEH-loh-fhunh) // xylophone

xénon (ZEH-nhonh) // xenon

The letter "Y" (ee-grehk)...

Yves (eevh) // Yves

yaourt (YEH-oh-ahtt) // yogurt

yacht (yohtt) // yacht

The letter "Z" (zhed)...

zèbre (ZEH-bah) // zebra

zoomer (ZOOH-mhey) // (to) zoom

zéro (ZEH-rhoh) // zero

The combination "ai" (pronounced "ah" or "eh")...

pain (pahnh) // bread

faire (fhehr) // (to) do, (to) make

The combination "au" (pronounced "oh")...

autobus (OH-toh-byoos) // bus

aussi (OH-see) // also

The combination "ch" (pronounced "sh")...

chien (shiyan) // dog

chaud (shoh) // hot

The combination "eau" (pronounced "oh" or "oo")...

château (SHAH-toh) // castle

beaucoup (BOO-ku) // a lot

The combination "ei" (pronounced "eh")...

neige (nehzh) // snow

treize (tghrehz) // thirteen

The combination "eu" (pronounced "uh" or "oo")...

fleur (fluhrh) // flower

heureux (OO-rhuh) // happy

The combination "gn" (pronounced "ny")...

montagne (MOHN-tah-ny) // mountain

magnifique (MHA-nyi-feek) // magnificent

The combination "ill" (pronounced "eeh")...

fille (FEEH-yeh) // girl, daughter

brillant (BHREEH-yon) // brilliant, bright

The combination "oi" (pronounced "wha")...

roi (rwhah) // king

voir (vwhah) // (to) see

The combination "ou" (pronounced "oo")...

jour (jyoorh) // day

doux (dooh) // mild, soft, sweet

The combination "ph" (pronounced "f")...

phrase (fhrahz) // sentence

philosophique (FEE-loh-zoh-feehk) // philosophical

The combination "qu" (pronounced "kh")...

question (KHES-chyon) // question

quotidien (kho-tee-dee-AHN) // daily

The combination "th" (pronounced "t")...

théâtre (TEY-ah-tgh) // theater

thermique (TEYR-meekh) // thermal

Welcome to Paris...

So, Where Exactly Is Paris Located?

Paris is the largest city, as well as the capital city, within the country of France, which is located in Western Europe and plays a prominent role in the world in many ways. France is comprised of eighteen administrative regions and Paris is located within the northernly Île-de-France administrative region. Île-de-France itself is divided into eight departments and Paris is a department of its own. The city of Paris is also a municipality of its own, which is then partitioned into twenty numerical municipal districts, or arrondissements, from the 1st arrondissement at the city center which spirals outwards and clockwise, much like a snail's shell, to the 20th arrondissement which is located in the eastern outskirts of the city.

Cities which share a common latitude also more or less share common daylight hours across the seasons. The latitude of

Paris is 48.86 degrees North, which places this French city a similar distance north of the Earth's equator as Germany's Baden-Württemberg and Bavaria, or the northernmost states in the United States such as Washington, Montana, and Minnesota, or Russia's Sakhalin Island, just north of Japan. Being in the northern hemisphere, the shortest daylight hours in Paris typically occur in late December with sunrise at around 8:40am and sunset just before 5pm for just 8 hours and 15 minutes of light. The longest daylight hours in Paris typically occur in late June with sunrise at around 5:47am and sunset just before 10pm for an incredible 16 hours and 10 minutes of light. That's quite a big difference!

What Languages Do People Speak in Paris?

French is both the official language as well as the most commonly spoken language, by far, within the city of Paris, with 95.8% of the population capable of speaking French as of the year 2024 according to the Language Knowledge EU website.

Other languages most commonly spoken in Paris include English with 24.6% of the population comfortably speaking the language, followed by Spanish (7.8%), German (3.3%), Arabic (3.1%), Italian (2.5%), and Portuguese (1.8%). There are many other less commonly spoken languages abound in Paris as well from all across the world.

Really, Why Is Paris Such a Popular Tourist Destination?

Paris is truly a cosmopolitan city with something delightful for everybody, whether it's seeing the famous attractions and historical landmarks while enjoying world-class restaurants and bakeries, shopping for high-end to more affordable French fashion goods and souvenirs while walking past the many manifestations of an artistic city, or finding oneself in a romantic getaway and catching the sparkling lights of the Eiffel Tower after dusk.

Because Paris is one of Europe's major cities, it also serves as an extremely convenient point of access to not only to other destinations within France, like Aix-en-Provence, Lyon, Bordeaux, Strasbourg, and much more, but also to any other major city in the world via the highly abundant airline and railway network systems. Thus, one can come to Paris to not only experience and revel in its unparalleled offerings, but also to commute easily, quickly, and affordably to other destinations or simply back home to plan the next great adventure.

Charles de Gaulle Airport

The City of Paris

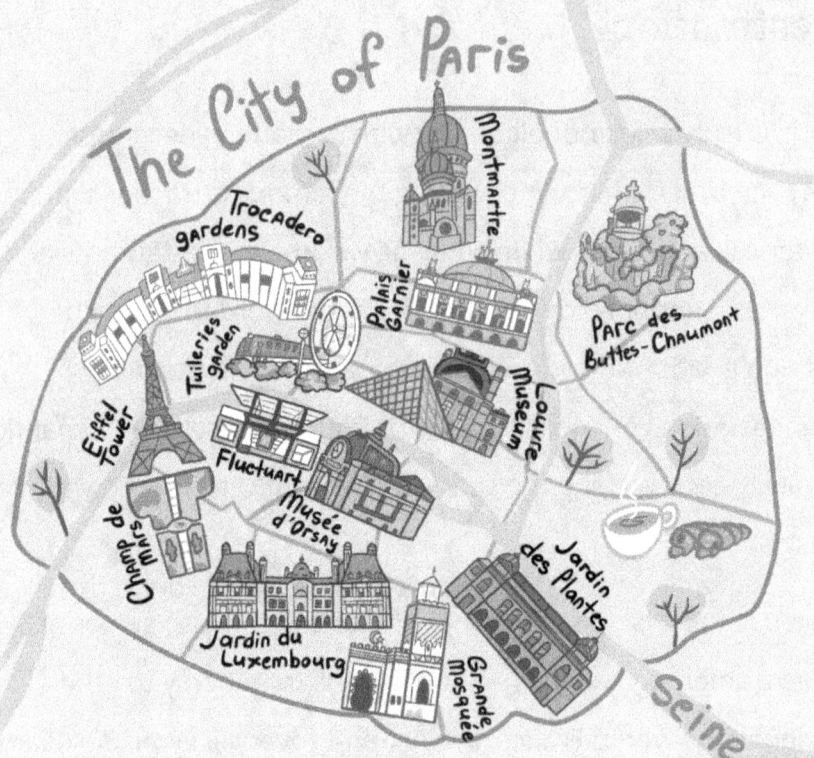

Montmartre

Trocadero
gardens

Palais
Garnier

Parc des
Buttes-Chaumont

Tuileries
garden

Louvre
Museum

Eiffel
Tower

Fluctuart

Musée
d'Orsay

Jardin
des Plantes

Champ de
Mars

Jardin du
Luxembourg

Grande
Mosquée

Seine

Orly Airport

Chapter 1

"Jules and His Cat, Mistigri" //
"Jules et son chat Mistigri"

Photo of Eiffel Tower at night by Andrey Emelyanenko.

Featured Vocabulary

The following vocabulary are presented in order of appearance...

à Paris: in Paris

il y a: there is

est étudiant: is a student

grand et mince: tall and slim

il a: he has

un pouvoir magique: a magical power

la personne qui: the person who

le conduit: drives it

un chat gris: a gray cat

le chat s'appelle: the cat is called

dit à: says to

quelqu'un: someone

un problème: a problem

et alors: and then

un jour: one day

pour l'instant: for the time being

tout va bien: all is well

on se retrouve ce soir: see you tonight

bien sûr: of course

dans la nuit: in the night

à l'entrée: at the entrance

l'épaule de Jules: Jules' shoulder

soudain: suddenly

touristes américains: American tourists

je peux: I can

poliment: politely

nous cherchons: we're looking for

le père: the father

suivez-moi: follow me

il les conduit: he leads them

ligne 6 du métro: metro line 6

la famille: the family

une fleur: a flower

je vous en prie: you're welcome

regardent les lumières: look at the lights

ils dînent au: they dine at the

du chevreuil avec des airelles: venison with cranberries

le propriétaire connaît: the owner knows

une fois: one time

donc: therefore

toujours le bienvenu: always welcome

dans ce café réputé: in this famous café

une bonne journée: a good day

aujourd'hui: today

oui: yes

c'était: it was

Short Story: "Jules and His Cat, Mistigri"

À Paris, il y a un jeune homme blond. Il s'appelle Jules.

In Paris, there is a young, blonde man. His name is Jules.

Jules est étudiant. Il étudie l'histoire. Il est grand et mince.

Jules is a student. He studies history. He is tall and slim.

Il a un scooter rouge brillant. Le scooter a un pouvoir magique. Il rend invisible la personne qui le conduit.

He has a shiny, red scooter. The scooter has a magical power. It makes the person who drives it invisible.

Jules a un chat gris. Le chat s'appelle Mistigri.

Jules has a gray cat. The cat is called Mistigri.

C'est un chat qui parle. Il a des yeux malicieux et un joli museau. Mistigri dit à Jules quand quelqu'un a un problème et alors Jules vient aider.

He is a cat who talks. He has mischievous eyes and a pretty muzzle. Mistigri says to Jules when someone has a problem and then Jules comes to help.

Un jour, Jules décide de s'amuser. Il dit à Mistigri : "Je pars

avec mon scooter !".

One day, Jules decides to have fun. He says to Mistigri, "I'm leaving with my scooter!".

Mistigri répond : "Amusez-vous bien ! Pour l'instant, tout va bien à Paris !".

Mistigri replies, "Have fun! For the time being, all is well in Paris!".

"On se retrouve ce soir à la Tour Eiffel", dit Jules.

"See you tonight at the Eiffel Tower," says Jules.

"Bien sûr !", répond Mistigri.

"Of course!", replies Mistigri.

Le soir arrive. Jules va à la Tour Eiffel.

Evening arrives. Jules goes to the Eiffel Tower.

La Tour Eiffel brille dans la nuit. Mistigri attend Jules à l'entrée. Le chat saute sur l'épaule de Jules.

The Eiffel Tower shines in the night. Mistigri is waiting for Jules at the entrance. The cat jumps on Jules' shoulder.

Soudain, Jules voit une famille de touristes américains. Ils se disputent. "Bonjour, je peux vous aider ?", demande-t-il

poliment.

Suddenly, Jules sees a family of American tourists. They're arguing. "Hello, can I help you?", he asks politely.

"Nous cherchons le métro," répond le père. "Nous voulons aller au Musée de l'Illusion."

"We're looking for the metro," replies the father. "We want to go to the Museum of Illusions."

"Suivez-moi," dit Jules. Il les conduit à la station Bir-Hakeim, sur la ligne 6 du métro.

"Follow me," says Jules. He leads them to the Bir-Hakeim station, on the metro line 6.

La famille dit : "Merci beaucoup !". Leur jolie fille lui donne une fleur.

The family says, "Thank you very much!". Their pretty daughter gives him a flower.

Jules répond : "Je vous en prie !". Jules est heureux d'avoir aidé.

Jules replies, "You're welcome!". Jules is happy to have helped.

Jules et Mistigri regardent les lumières de Paris un moment.

Puis ils dînent au café Le Jules Verne. Jules commande du chevreuil avec des airelles.

Jules and Mistigri look at the lights of Paris for a moment. Then they dine at the café, Le Jules Verne. Jules orders venison with cranberries.

Le propriétaire connaît Jules et Mistigri. Une fois, ils l'ont beaucoup aidé. Donc Mistigri est toujours le bienvenu dans ce café réputé.

The owner knows Jules and Mistigri. One time, they helped him a lot. Therefore, Mistigri is always welcome in this famous café.

Mistigri demande : "Alors, une bonne journée ?".

Mistigri asks, "So, a good day?".

Jules répond : "Oui, nous avons aidé des gens aujourd'hui. Donc oui, c'était une bonne journée."

Jules replies, "Yes, we've helped people today. Therefore, yes, it was a good day."

Chapter 2
"The Attractions of the Louvre" // "Les attractions du Louvre"

Photo of the Louvre pyramid by Karel Miragaya.

Featured Vocabulary

The following vocabulary are presented in order of appearance...

et son chat: and his cat

roulent sur leur: riding on their

à Paris: in Paris

il fait beau: the weather is nice

ils s'arrêtent au: they stop at the

pour visiter: to visit

veut boire: wants to drink

le célèbre: the famous

reçoit toujours: always receives

j'aime: I like

est comme: is like

ou: or

magnifique: beautiful

brille comme un diamant: sparkles like a diamond

avant d'aller au: before going to the

ils voient: they see

un vieil homme: an old man

perdu et inquiet: lost and worried

cet homme: this man

bien sûr: of course

gare le scooter: parks the scooter

avez-vous besoin: do you need

l'homme: the man

ne vous inquiétez pas: don't worry

je connais: I know

allons au: let's go to the

quand: when

en robe blanche: in a white dress

elle mange: she is eating

la femme: the woman

ici comme convenu: here as agreed

où d'autre: where else

près du Louvre: near the Louvre

qui est: who is

il m'a aidé: he has helped me

à te retrouver: to find you

une ganache à la framboise: a raspberry ganache

également: also

pour Mistigri: for Mistigri

ensuite: afterwards

ensemble: together

avec joie: with the greatest pleasure

Short Story: "The Attractions of the Louvre"

Jules et son chat Mistigri roulent sur leur scooter magique à Paris. Il fait beau et chaud.

Jules and his cat Mistigri are riding on their magic scooter in Paris.

The weather is nice and warm.

Ils s'arrêtent au Musée du Louvre pour visiter la Maison du Chocolat. Jules veut boire un café avec le célèbre ganache à la framboise. Mistigri y reçoit toujours de la crème fraîche.

They stop at the Louvre Museum to visit the Maison du Chocolat. Jules wants to drink a coffee with the famous raspberry ganache. Mistigri always receives fresh cream there.

Jules dit : "J'aime la pyramide en verre. Elle est comme du futur ou d'un conte de fées."

Jules says, "I like the glass pyramid. It's like from the future or from a fairy tale."

Mistigri dit : "Oui, elle est magnifique ! Elle brille comme un diamant."

Mistigri says, "Yes, it's beautiful! It sparkles like a diamond."

Mais avant d'aller au café, ils voient un vieil homme perdu et inquiet.

But before going to the café, they see a lost and worried old man.

Mistigri dit : "Aidons cet homme."

Mistigri says, "Let's help this man."

Jules répond : "Oui, bien sûr !".

Jules replies, "Yes, of course!".

Jules gare le scooter au Parking Indigo Paris Louvre Samaritaine.

Jules parks the scooter at the Parking Indigo Paris Louvre Samaritaine.

Il va voir le vieil homme.

He goes to see the old man.

"Monsieur, avez-vous besoin d'aide ?", demande Jules.

"Sir, do you need any help?", asks Jules.

"Ma femme Rose a disparu ! Nous voulions voir l'original de 'La Liberté guidant le peuple,'" répond l'homme.

"My wife, Rose, has disappeared! We wanted to see the original of 'Liberty Leading the People,'" replies the man.

Jules dit : "Ne vous inquiétez pas, je connais bien Paris. Allons au café et je réfléchirai à un plan."

Jules says, "Don't worry, I know Paris well. Let's go to the café and I'll think of a plan."

Quand ils entrent, ils voient une belle dame âgée en robe blanche. Elle mange du praliné.

When they enter, they see a beautiful, elderly lady in a white dress. She is eating pralines.

"Rose ?", crie l'homme.

"Rose?", shouts the man.

La femme se retourne.

The woman turns around.

"Nicolas ! Je vous attends ici comme convenu !".

"Nicolas! I'm waiting for you here as agreed!".

Jules rit. "Bien sûr ! Où d'autre pourrait-on se perdre près du Louvre ?".

Jules laughs. "Of course! Where else could one get lost near the Louvre?".

"Qui est ce jeune homme ?", demande Rose.

"Who is this young man?", asks Rose.

"Mon sauveur, il m'a aidé à te retrouver !", répond Nicolas.

"My savior, he has helped me to find you!", replies Nicolas.

Nicolas commande une ganache à la framboise pour Jules. Il commande également du café, du chocolat et de la crème pour Mistigri.

Nicolas orders a raspberry ganache for Jules. He also orders coffee, chocolate and cream for Mistigri.

Ensuite, ils visitent ensemble le musée avec joie.

Afterwards, they visit the museum together with the greatest pleasure.

Chapter 3

"A Beautiful Day" // "Une belle journée"

Photo of Buttes-Chaumont Park by Laurent Davoust.

Featured Vocabulary

The following vocabulary are presented in order of appearance...

une journée ensoleillée: a sunny day

un café: a coffee

une mousse au chocolat maison: a homemade chocolate mousse

un bol en métal: a metal bowl

avec de l'huile et du sel: with oil and salt

pour deux: for two

les jolies rues: the pretty streets

tout à coup: all of a sudden

Mistigri lève la tête: Mistigri raises his head

portefeuille: wallet

une femme triste: a sad woman

qui a perdu: who has lost

cartes: cards

argent: money

n'est pas: is not

une habitante locale: a local resident

offre toujours de la crème: always offers cream

elle fait aussi: she also makes

merveilleux: wonderful

partout dans les environs: everywhere in the surroundings

grâce à: thanks to

son scooter magique: his magic scooter

heureusement: fortunately

sous un banc: under a bench

près du: near the

les oiseaux: the birds

une baguette fraîche: a fresh baguette

est vert: is green

c'est pourquoi: which is why

ne l'a pas vu: didn't see it

de plus: moreover

le vent: the wind

le prend et le rend: takes it and returns it

merci beaucoup: thank you so much

même: even

je suis content: I'm glad

est confortablement installé: is comfortably seated

le panier du scooter: the scooter basket

est presque aussi rose: is almost as pink

préféré: favorite

s'étire paresseusement: stretches lazily

toi et ta: you and your

bien sûr que non: of course not

je pense aussi à: I'm also thinking of

le soleil parisien: the Parisian sun

Short Story: "A Beautiful Day"

Par une journée ensoleillée, Jules boit un café sur les Champs-Élysées.

On a sunny day, Jules is drinking a coffee on the Champs-Élysées.

Il savoure une mousse au chocolat maison. On la sert dans un bol en métal avec de l'huile et du sel. C'est un café pour deux, et Jules est là avec son chat Mistigri.

He savors a homemade chocolate mousse. It's served in a metal bowl with oil and salt. It's a café for two, and Jules is there with his cat Mistigri.

Ils regardent les jolies rues du 18ème arrondissement de Paris.

They look at the pretty streets of Paris's 18th arrondissement.

Tout à coup, Mistigri lève la tête de sa crème et dit : "Jules, une femme a perdu son portefeuille au Parc des Buttes-Chaumont !".

All of a sudden, Mistigri raises his head from his cream and says, "Jules, a woman has lost her wallet at the Parc des Buttes-Chaumont!".

Jules s'approche et voit une femme triste. C'est Madame Dupont, qui a perdu son portefeuille avec ses cartes et son argent.

Jules approaches and sees a sad woman. It's Mrs. Dupont, who has lost her wallet with her cards and money.

Elle n'est pas une touriste. Elle est une habitante locale. Madame Dupont offre toujours de la crème à Mistigri. Elle fait aussi de merveilleux croissants.

She's not a tourist. She's a local resident. Mrs. Dupont always offers cream to Mistigri. She also makes wonderful croissants.

Jules cherche partout dans les environs. Grâce à sa vigilance, il trouve le portefeuille. Son scooter magique l'aide dans sa recherche.

Jules searches everywhere in the surroundings. Thanks to his vigilance, he finds the wallet. His magic scooter helps in his search.

Heureusement, le portefeuille n'a pas été volé. Il était tombé sous un banc.

Fortunately, the wallet wasn't stolen. It had fallen under a bench.

Madame Dupont était assise là, près du Lac des Minimes. Elle nourrissait les oiseaux avec une baguette fraîche.

Mrs. Dupont was sitting there, near the Lac des Minimes. She was feeding the birds with a fresh baguette.

Le portefeuille est vert, c'est pourquoi Madame Dupont ne l'a pas vu. De plus, le vent l'a soufflé sous le banc voisin.

The wallet is green, which is why Mrs. Dupont didn't see it. Moreover, the wind blew it under the nearby bench.

Jules le prend et le rend à Madame Dupont.

Jules takes it and returns it to Mrs. Dupont.

"Oh, merci beaucoup !", s'exclame-t-elle. "Mais comment as-tu fait ? Je ne t'ai même pas vu !".

"Oh, thank you so much!", she exclaims. "But how did you do it? I didn't even see you!".

Jules sourit et dit : "Celui qui fait de bonnes actions ne doit pas être vu, madame. Je suis content d'avoir pu aider."

Jules smiles and says, "One who does good deeds must not be seen, ma'am. I'm glad to have been able to help."

Mistigri est confortablement installé dans le panier du scooter.

Mistigri is comfortably seated in the scooter basket.

"Mistigri, regarde comme le ciel est beau aujourd'hui !", Jules dit.

"Mistigri, look how beautiful the sky is today!", Jules says.

"Miaou... Il est presque aussi rose que mon pâté de saumon préféré." Mistigri s'étire paresseusement.

"Meow... It is almost as pink as my favorite salmon pâté." Mistigri stretches lazily.

"Toi et ta nourriture ! Tu ne penses vraiment qu'à ça ?", Jules rit.

"You and your food! Is that really all you think about?", Jules laughs.

"Bien sûr que non. Je pense aussi à me prélasser sous le soleil parisien !".

"Of course not. I'm also thinking of lounging under the Parisian sun!".

Chapter 4

"Mr. Invisible" // "Monsieur invisible"

Photo of the Luxembourg Gardens by Pascale Gueret.

Featured Vocabulary

The following vocabulary are presented in order of appearance...

un matin: one morning

une nouvelle mission: a new mission

un enfant perdu: a lost child

s'habille et se lave: gets dressed and washes up

rapidement: quickly

comme toujours: as always

déjà prêt: already ready

brille de rouge: glows red

au soleil: in the sun

sur les rues pavées: on the cobbled streets

passant devant: in front of

l'odeur: the smell

épices françaises: French spices

chariot de glaces: ice cream cart

le petit Paul: Little Paul

une glace aux noisettes: a hazelnut ice cream

ne t'inquiète pas: don't worry

à ta maman: to your mommy

son talent incroyable: his incredible talent

la mère de Paul: Paul's mother

soulagée: relieved

monsieur invisible: Mr. Invisible

derrière: behind

des rires et des murmures: laughter and whispers

tu sais: you know

c'est facile: it is easy

quand: when

et surtout: and especially

les embouteillages: (the) traffic jams

le jardin: the garden

lui et Mistigri: he and Mistigri

les lampadaires: the street lamps

dans ces moments-là: in times like these

je comprends pourquoi: I understand why

la ville de l'amour: the city of love

parce que: because

français: French

ici: here

non: no

chaque soir: every evening

si confortablement: so comfortably

encore plus: even more

un morceau de: a piece of

peut-être: perhaps

Short Story: "Mr. Invisible"

Un matin, Mistigri réveille Jules. Une nouvelle mission

l'attend.

One morning, Mistigri wakes up Jules. A new mission awaits him.

"Jules, il y a un enfant perdu au Jardin du Luxembourg," dit Mistigri.

"Jules, there's a lost child at the Luxembourg Gardens," says Mistigri.

Jules s'habille et se lave rapidement. Mistigri, comme toujours, est déjà prêt.

Jules gets dressed and washes up quickly. Mistigri, as always, is already ready.

Le scooter magique brille de rouge au soleil. Ils roulent sur les rues pavées, passant devant L'Arpège. L'odeur des épices françaises emplit l'air.

The magic scooter glows red in the sun. They ride on the cobbled streets, passing in front of L'Arpège. The smell of French spices fills the air.

Près d'un chariot de glaces, ils trouvent le petit Paul. Il regarde autour de lui, perdu, mais savoure une glace aux noisettes.

Near an ice cream cart, they find Little Paul. He looks around, lost, but enjoys a hazelnut ice cream.

"Ne t'inquiète pas, Paul, nous allons te ramener à ta maman. Suis ma voix," dit Jules. Paul ne le voit pas.

"Don't worry, Paul, we will bring you back to your mommy. Follow my voice," says Jules. Paul doesn't see him.

Mistigri, avec son talent incroyable, guide Jules à travers le labyrinthe de buissons et de statues.

Mistigri, with his incredible talent, guides Jules through the maze of bushes and statues.

"Paul !", crie une femme. C'est la mère de Paul, soulagée de retrouver son fils.

"Paul!", cries a woman. It's Paul's mother, relieved to find her son again.

"Merci, monsieur invisible," dit Paul en souriant.

"Thank you, Mr. Invisible," says Paul with a smile.

Jules et Mistigri s'en vont. Ils entendent derrière eux des rires et des murmures sur la magie.

Jules and Mistigri leave. Behind them, they hear laughter and whispers about magic.

"Tu sais, Mistigri, c'est facile d'aider quand on a des assistants magiques," dit Jules.

"You know, Mistigri, it is easy to help when we have magical assistants," says Jules.

"Oui, et surtout quand on peut éviter les embouteillages !", ajoute Mistigri.

"Yes, and especially when we can avoid traffic jams!", adds Mistigri.

Jusqu'au soir, Jules et Mistigri se promènent au Jardin du Luxembourg. Jules connaît bien le jardin. Il roule sur des chemins où personne ne marche.

Until the evening, Jules and Mistigri take a stroll through the Luxembourg Gardens. Jules knows the garden well. He rides on paths where no one walks.

Lui et Mistigri passent devant les statues. Il y en a 106 au Jardin du Luxembourg !

He and Mistigri pass in front of the statues. There are 106 of them at the Luxembourg Gardens!

Quand les lampadaires s'allument, Jules dit : "Tu sais, dans ces

moments-là, je comprends pourquoi on appelle Paris la ville de l'amour."

When the street lamps come on, Jules says, "You know, in times like these, I understand why we call Paris the city of love."

"Parce que même les chats parlent français ici ?", Mistigri ronronne.

"Because even the cats speak French here?", Mistigri purrs.

"Non. C'est parce que chaque soir se termine si confortablement ici."

"No. It's because every evening ends so comfortably here."

"Alors, finissons-le encore plus confortablement. Un morceau de camembert, peut-être ?", Mistigri dit.

"Then, let's finish it even more comfortably. A piece of Camembert, perhaps?", Mistigri says.

"Oh, Mistigri, tu es incorrigible !", Jules rit.

"Oh, Mistigri, you're incorrigible!", Jules laughs.

Chapter 5

"The Clown's Smile" // "Le sourire du clown"

Photo of view from Montmartre by Alberto Mazza.

Featured Vocabulary

The following vocabulary are presented in order of appearance...

dans les rues: through the streets

ce clown là-bas: that clown over there

semble avoir: seems to have

son sourire: his smile

en effet: indeed

dans sa main: in his hand

ce qui se passe: what's going on

ils descendent du: they get off the

pour le clown: to the clown

de nulle part: out of nowhere

Monsieur le Clown: Mr. Clown

pourquoi êtes-vous: why are you

d'où: from where

mes ballons: my balloons

sans: without

je ne peux pas: I can't

mon spectacle: my show

dans les arbres du: in the trees of the

un groupe d'oiseaux colorés: a group of colorful birds

à Paris: in Paris

de plus près: up close

accrochés à l'arbre: hanging on the tree

avec moi: with me

quel gentil chat: what a kind cat

ils disparaissent tous: they all disappear

très vite: very quickly

ils réapparaissent: they reappear

le clown heureux: the happy clown

stupéfait: stunned

il offre à: he offers to

deux des: two of the

nous sommes contents: we are happy

votre sourire: your smile

à la fin de la journée: at the end of the day

le croissant spécial: the special croissant

fromage de chèvre: goat cheese

figues: figs

avec des noisettes: with hazelnuts

quelle journée: what a day

demain: tomorrow

encore plus: even more

Short Story: "The Clown's Smile"

Par une journée ensoleillée, Jules et son chat Mistigri se promènent dans les rues de Montmartre.

On a sunny day, Jules and his cat Mistigri take a stroll through the streets of Montmartre.

"Jules, regarde !", dit Mistigri. "Ce clown là-bas semble avoir perdu son sourire."

"Jules, look!", says Mistigri. "That clown over there seems to have lost his smile."

En effet, ils voient un clown triste assis sur un banc. Il tient son nez rouge dans sa main.

Indeed, they see a sad clown sitting on a bench. He's holding his red nose in his hand.

"Allons voir ce qui se passe," dit Jules.

"Let's see what's going on," says Jules.

Ils s'approchent de lui. Ils descendent du scooter magique. Pour le clown, ils apparaissent simplement de nulle part.

They approach him. They get off the magic scooter. To the clown, they simply appear out of nowhere.

"Bonjour, Monsieur le Clown, pourquoi êtes-vous si triste ?", demande Jules.

"Hello, Mr. Clown, why are you so sad?", asks Jules.

"Oh, d'où viens-tu ?!", s'exclame le clown. "Le vent a emporté mes ballons. Sans eux, je ne peux pas faire mon spectacle."

"Oh, where are you from?!", exclaims the clown. "The wind blew my balloons away. Without them, I can't do my show."

Jules et le clown discutent. Mistigri observe les oiseaux dans les arbres du Square Louise Michel.

Jules and the clown talk. Mistigri observes the birds in the trees of the Square Louise Michel.

Soudain, Mistigri voit un groupe d'oiseaux colorés dans un arbre.

Suddenly, Mistigri sees a group of colorful birds in a tree.

"Je n'ai jamais vu d'oiseaux aussi brillants à Paris !", s'étonne Mistigri. Il court pour les voir de plus près.

"I've never seen such bright birds in Paris!", wonders Mistigri. He runs to see them up close.

Ce ne sont pas des oiseaux ! Ce sont les ballons du clown ! Ils sont accrochés à l'arbre. Mistigri retourne vers Jules.

These are not birds! These are the clown's balloons! They're hanging from the tree. Mistigri returns towards Jules.

"Viens avec moi !", appelle le chat.

"Come with me!", calls the cat.

"Ah, quel gentil chat tu es !", s'étonne le clown.

"Ah, what a kind cat you are!", exclaims the clown.

Jules saute sur son scooter. Mistigri bondit sur son épaule. Et ils disparaissent tous ensemble.

Jules jumps on his scooter. Mistigri leaps onto his shoulder. And they all disappear together.

Très vite, ils réapparaissent devant le clown.

Very quickly, they reappear in front of the clown.

Le clown heureux est stupéfait. Il offre à Jules et Mistigri deux des ballons les plus brillants.

The happy clown is stunned. He offers to Jules and Mistigri two of the brightest balloons.

"Nous sommes contents de vous avoir rendu votre sourire !", dit Jules.

"We are happy for having returned your smile!", says Jules.

À la fin de la journée, Jules et Mistigri sont assis au Café de Luce. Jules commande le croissant spécial au fromage de chèvre et aux figues avec des noisettes, et Mistigri un croissant aux escargots au persil.

At the end of the day, Jules and Mistigri are sitting at Café de Luce. Jules orders the special goat cheese and fig croissant with hazelnuts, and Mistigri a croissant with snails and parsley.

"Quelle journée pleine d'aventures !", dit Jules.

"What a day full of adventure!", says Jules.

"Oui, et demain nous en vivrons encore plus," ronronne Mistigri.

"Yes, and tomorrow we'll experience even more," purrs Mistigri.

Chapter 6

"The Young Artist" // "La jeune artiste"

Photo of a ham, cheese, and tomato tartine by Larisa Matrosova.

Featured Vocabulary

The following vocabulary are presented in order of appearance...

de nouveau: once again

personne ne: no one

car: because

fontaine: fountain

une petite fille: a little girl

qui: who

les enfants: children

ne devraient pas: should not

il s'arrête: he stops

ses pinceaux: his brushes

il peut: he can

sûrement: surely

qu'ils étaient: that they were

maintenant: now

abîmés: damaged

j'ai peur: I'm afraid

je suis sûr: I'm sure

sera: will be

tu deviennes aussi: you also become

allons-y: let's go

il marmonne: he mumbles

quelque chose: something // anything

en fouillant dans: while rummaging through

une boîte: a box

c'est toi: it's you

n'arrive pas à imaginer: can't come to imagine

où: where

pour peindre: to paint

un tableau: a picture

serais-tu: would you be

très: very

en colère: angry

tout: everything

me demander: ask me

avant de prendre: before taking

la prochaine fois: the next time

au café voisin: to the nearby café

une tartine: a toast

jambon: ham

fromage: cheese

est née: was born

pour ne pas: so as not to

Short Story: "The Young Artist"

Jules et Mistigri sont de nouveau au Jardin du Luxembourg. Personne ne les voit car ils roulent sur un scooter magique.

Jules and Mistigri are once again at the Luxembourg Gardens. No one sees them because they are riding on a magic scooter.

Ils admirent la fontaine Médicis.

They admire the Medici Fountain.

Soudain, ils voient une petite fille qui pleure. C'est Sophie, la fille d'un artiste.

Suddenly, they see a little girl who is crying. It's Sophie, the daughter of an artist.

"Les enfants ne devraient pas pleurer !", dit Jules. Il s'arrête et descend du scooter. "Que se passe-t-il, Sophie ?".

"Children shouldn't cry!", says Jules. He stops and gets off from the scooter. "What's going on, Sophie?".

"Mon père a perdu ses pinceaux."

"My father has lost his brushes."

"Il peut sûrement acheter de nouveaux pinceaux, Sophie. Ne t'inquiète pas !", la rassure Jules.

"He can surely buy new brushes, Sophie. Don't worry!", Jules reassures her.

"Oui, mais c'est moi qui ai pris les pinceaux pour dessiner. Je ne savais pas qu'ils étaient spéciaux. Maintenant ils sont

abîmés. Et j'ai peur de l'avouer à mon père."

"Yes, but it was me who took the brushes to draw. I didn't know that they were special. Now they're damaged. And I'm afraid to admit it to my father."

"Oh, je suis sûr qu'il sera juste content. Je l'ai entendu dire qu'il veut que tu deviennes aussi une artiste ! Allons-y ensemble."

"Oh, I'm sure that he'll be just happy. I've heard him say that he wants that you also become an artist! Let's go together."

Ils s'approchent de l'artiste Thomas. Il marmonne quelque chose en fouillant dans une boîte de pinceaux.

They approach the artist, Thomas. He mumbles something while rummaging through a box of brushes.

"Bonjour, Thomas !", dit Jules.

"Hello, Thomas!", says Jules.

"Ah, c'est toi Jules, comme toujours avec ton chat. Oh, et Sophie est avec vous."

"Ah, it's you, Jules, as always with your cat. Oh, and Sophie is with you."

"J'ai entendu que tu avais perdu tes pinceaux."

"I've heard you had lost your brushes."

"Oui, je n'arrive pas à imaginer où ils ont disparu !".

"Yes, I can't come to imagine where they have disappeared!".

"Et si tu apprenais qu'un jeune artiste les a pris pour peindre un tableau ? Mais il les a accidentellement abîmés. Serais-tu très en colère ?", demande Jules.

"And if you learned that a young artist has taken them to paint a picture? But he accidentally got them damaged. Would you be very angry?", asks Jules.

Thomas regarde Jules et sa fille. Il comprend tout.

Thomas looks at Jules and his daughter. He understands everything.

"Ah, bien sûr que non. Mais le jeune artiste devrait me demander avant de prendre quelque chose."

"Ah, of course not. But the young artist should ask me before taking anything."

"Je suis sûr que la prochaine fois, le jeune artiste te demandera conseil," dit Jules.

"I'm sure that the next time, the young artist will ask your advice," says Jules.

Ils vont tous ensemble au café voisin. Jules savoure un steak tartare et une tartine au jambon, fromage et tomates. Sophie commande un parfait.

They all go together to the nearby café. Jules enjoys a steak tartare and a toast with ham, cheese, and tomatoes. Sophie orders a parfait.

"Une excellente journée, où la jeune artiste est née," dit Jules.

"An excellent day, where the young artist was born," says Jules.

"Miaou," dit Mistigri, pour ne pas révéler qu'il sait parler.

"Meow," said Mistigri, so as not to reveal that he knows how to speak.

Chapter 7

"A Miracle in Paris" // "Un miracle à Paris"

Photo of a mille-feuille by Oleksandr Prokopenko.

Featured Vocabulary

The following vocabulary are presented in order of appearance...

au cœur de: in the heart of

près de: next to

frères artistes: artist brothers

tous les deux: both

un malentendu: a misunderstanding

pense que: thinks that

a vendu: has sold

peinture préférée: favorite painting

simplement oublié: simply forgotten

restauration: restoration

à se réconcilier: to reconcile

voici: here is

ils dégustent: they're tasting

délicieux: delicious

croissants frais: fresh croissants

il entend: he hears

entre: between

œuvres: artwork

seul: alone

tristement: sadly

je voulais: I wanted to

ton anniversaire: your birthday

ses yeux: his eyes

visite discrètement: discreetly visits

dans l'atelier: in the workshop

leurs mots: their words

un miracle parisien: a Parisian miracle

parfois: sometimes

il suffit: all it takes is

un repas: a meal

le garçon: the boy

depuis ce jour: since that day

ils croient: they believe

même si c'est: even if it is

la bonté: the kindness

un être invisible: an invisible being

Short Story: "A Miracle in Paris"

Au cœur de Paris, près de la Seine, vivent deux frères artistes, Pierre et Luc. Ils travaillent tous les deux à Fluctuart. Ils sont connus pour leurs magnifiques peintures.

In the heart of Paris, next to the Seine, live two artist brothers, Pierre and Luc. They both work at Fluctuart. They are known for their magnificent paintings.

Mais un jour, ils se disputent. Il y a eu un malentendu.

But one day, they are arguing. There was a misunderstanding.

Pierre pense que Luc a vendu leur peinture préférée sans lui demander. Et Luc croit que Pierre l'a perdu. Pierre a simplement oublié à qui il a donné la peinture pour

restauration.

Pierre thinks that Luc has sold their favorite painting without asking him. And Luc believes that Pierre has lost it. Pierre has simply forgotten to whom he has given the painting for restoration.

Un jour, Jules et Mistigri aident les frères à se réconcilier.

One day, Jules and Mistigri help the brothers to reconcile.

Voici comment. Les frères sont au Café Fluctuat Nec Mergitur. Ils dégustent un délicieux mille-feuille.

Here's how. The brothers are at the Café Fluctuat Nec Mergitur. They're tasting a delicious mille-feuille.

Jules passe pour acheter des croissants frais. Ce café vend sa variété préférée. Il entend une nouvelle dispute entre les frères.

Jules comes by to buy fresh croissants. This café sells his favorite variety. He hears a new argument between the brothers.

"Je ne comprends pas ! Je n'ai jamais vendu nos œuvres seul," dit Luc tristement.

"I don't understand! I have never sold our artwork alone," Luc says sadly.

"Je ne l'ai pas perdu ! Je voulais le restaurer pour ton anniversaire," répond Pierre. Ses yeux montrent du regret.

"I haven't lost it! I wanted to restore it for your birthday," replies Pierre. His eyes show regret.

Jules utilise son scooter invisible. Il visite discrètement les ateliers de restauration. Dans l'atelier de La Réserve des Arts, Jules voit la peinture des frères.

Jules uses his invisible scooter. He discreetly visits the restoration workshops. In the workshop of La Réserve des Arts, Jules sees the brothers' painting.

Il le prend. Et soudain, la peinture apparaît sur la table. Quand ils voient la peinture, ils perdent leurs mots.

He takes it. And suddenly, the painting appears on the table. When they see the painting, they lose their words.

"C'est notre peinture ! Comment est-il revenu ?", s'exclame Pierre.

"That's our painting! How did it come back?", exclaims Pierre.

"C'est un miracle parisien," dit Luc en souriant.

"It's a Parisian miracle," says Luc with a smile.

Mistigri miaule : "Parfois, il suffit d'un peu de magie et de compréhension pour résoudre un malentendu."

Mistigri meows: "Sometimes, all it takes is a bit of magic and understanding can resolve a misunderstanding."

Les frères s'embrassent. Leur relation se répare. Ils offrent un repas à Jules et son chat. Ils le font par joie. Les frères ne savent pas que le garçon et le chat les ont aidés.

The brothers embrace. Their relationship repairs itself. They offer a meal to Jules and his cat. They do so out of joy. The brothers don't know that the boy and the cat have helped them.

Depuis ce jour, Pierre et Luc travaillent à nouveau ensemble.

Since that day, Pierre and Luc are working together again.

L'atmosphère magique de Paris les inspire. Ils croient aux miracles et à la bonté. Même si c'est la bonté d'un être invisible.

The magical atmosphere of Paris inspires them. They believe in miracles and kindness. Even if it's the kindness of an invisible being.

Chapter 8

"The Mysterious Letter" // "La lettre mystérieuse"

Photo of Trocadero Gardens by Anastasija Jarmolowicz.

Featured Vocabulary

The following vocabulary are presented in order of appearance...

matin ensoleillé: sunny morning

la Tour Eiffel: the Eiffel Tower

ils admirent: they admire

ils observent: they observe

l'eau: the water

Jardin du Trocadéro: Trocadero Gardens

tartare de bœuf: beef tartare

pommes de terre: potatoes

ail: garlic

œufs bio: organic eggs

herbes fraîches: fresh herbs

d'en haut: from above

délicatement: delicately

est écrit: is written

adresse de retour: return address

de trouver: to find

le plus gentil: the kindest

les bonnes actions: the good deeds

Parisiens: Parsians

un sans-abri: a homeless person

la cathédrale Notre-Dame: the Notre-Dame Cathedral

ensuite: and then

une personne âgée: an elderly person

à traverser la rue: to cross the street

le Quartier Latin: the Latin Quarter

un ballon: a ball (large like a basketball)

coincé: stuck

un arbre: a tree

ne remarquent pas: don't notice

égaré: lost

la Basilique du Sacré-Cœur: the Sacré-Cœur Basilica

maître reconnaissant: grateful master

de mille feux: with a thousand lights

malgré: despite

n'arrivent pas à décider: can't come to decide

joyeux: happy

habitant: resident

on continuera: we will continue

la fenêtre: the window

légumes de saison: seasonal vegetables

pour lui-même: for himself

échalotes: shallots

un dîner: a dinner

certainement: certainly

cette lettre: this letter

absolument: absolutely

Short Story: "The Mysterious Letter"

Par un matin ensoleillé, Jules et Mistigri sont sur la Tour Eiffel. Ils admirent Paris. Ils observent l'eau qui danse dans les fontaines du Jardin du Trocadéro.

On a sunny morning, Jules and Mistigri are on the Eiffel Tower. They admire Paris. They observe the water dancing in the fountains of Trocadero Gardens.

Jules commande le tartare de bœuf avec des pommes de terre sautées, de l'ail et du thym. Mistigri déguste des œufs bio avec de la mayonnaise, une salade et des herbes fraîches.

Jules orders the beef tartare with sauteed potatoes, garlic, and thyme. Mistigri is enjoying the organic eggs with mayonnaise, a salad, and fresh herbs.

Soudain, une enveloppe tombe d'en haut. Jules la ramasse délicatement.

Suddenly, an envelope falls from above. Jules picks it up delicately.

Sur l'enveloppe est écrit : "Au plus gentil". Il n'y a pas d'adresse de retour.

On the envelope is written: "To the kindest". There's no return address.

Jules et Mistigri décident de trouver le plus gentil à Paris. Ils observent les bonnes actions des Parisiens.

Jules and Mistigri decide to find the kindest in Paris. They observe the good deeds of Parisians.

Ils voient un homme qui offre un repas à un sans-abri près de la cathédrale Notre-Dame.

They see a man who offers a meal to a homeless person next to the Notre-Dame Cathedral.

Ensuite, ils voient une femme qui aide une personne âgée à traverser la rue dans le Quartier Latin.

And then, they see a woman who helps an elderly person to cross the street in the Latin Quarter.

Il y a aussi un garçon qui récupère un ballon coincé dans un arbre pour un petit enfant au Jardin du Luxembourg.

There's also a boy who recovers a ball stuck in a tree for a little child at the Luxembourg Gardens.

Jules et Mistigri ne remarquent pas qu'ils aident aussi. Ils ramènent un touriste égaré à la Basilique du Sacré-Cœur. Ils

réunissent un chien perdu à son maître reconnaissant.

Jules and Mistigri don't notice that they're helping too. They bring back a lost tourist back to the Sacré-Cœur Basilica. They reunite a lost dog to its grateful master.

La journée touche à sa fin. Le cœur de Paris s'illumine de mille feux.

The day is drawing to an end. The heart of Paris dazzles with a thousand lights.

Malgré toutes les bonnes actions qu'ils ont vues, Jules et Mistigri n'arrivent pas à décider qui est le plus gentil.

Despite all the good deeds that they've seen, Jules and Mistigri can't come to decide who's the kindest.

Ils rentrent chez eux. Ils se sentent joyeux. Mais ils se demandent où trouver le plus gentil habitant de Paris.

They return home. They feel happy. But they wonder where to find the kindest resident in Paris.

"On continuera demain," se promettent-ils.

"We'll continue tomorrow," they promise each other.

Ils regardent par la fenêtre. Ils dînent sur le balcon.

They look out the window. They dine on the balcony.

Jules commande un confit de légumes de saison pour lui-même. Pour Mistigri, il commande un filet de bœuf avec échalotes et purée de pommes de terre. C'est un dîner parisien traditionnel.

Jules orders a confit of seasonal vegetables for himself. For Mistigri, he orders a filet of beef with shallots and mashed potatoes. It's a traditional Parisian dinner.

"La personne la plus gentille de Paris recevra certainement cette lettre !", dit Jules.

"The kindest person in Paris will certainly receive this letter!", says Jules.

"Absolument !", approuve Mistigri.

"Absolutely!", approves Mistigri.

Chapter 9

"A Future Artist's Notebook" //
"Le carnet d'un futur artiste"

Photo of a French apple tart by Anneke Schram.

Featured Vocabulary

The following vocabulary are presented in order of appearance...

une belle journée: a beautiful day

œuvres d'art: works of art

framboise: raspberry

lève les yeux: looks up

carnet de croquis: sketchbook

dit-elle: she says

mes dessins: my drawings

là: there

je m'appelle: my name is

cherchent: search for

le carnet: the notebook

partout: everywhere

le musée: the museum

la Joconde: the Mona Lisa

la galerie: the gallery

dit-il: he says

doucement: softly

est sous: is under

une vitrine: a showcase

coincé contre: stuck against

le mur: the wall

ses pattes: his paws

il pousse: he pushes

vers: towards

attend toujours: still waiting

très contente: very happy

elle montre: she shows

très bien: very well

je veux: I want

devenir: to become

le soir: the evening

ils vont au: they go to the

de là: from there

la pyramide: the pyramid

tarte aux pommes: apple tart

crème fraîche: fresh cream

ah bon: that's good

je croyais: I believed

qu'elle: that she

ils profitent de: they take advantage of

la magie: the magic

Short Story: "A Future Artist's Notebook"

C'est une belle journée. Jules et son chat Mistigri visitent le Louvre. Ils admirent les œuvres d'art.

It's a beautiful day. Jules and his cat Mistigri are visiting the Louvre. They admire the works of art.

Jules mange un macaron à la framboise. Mistigri mange du fromage brie.

Jules eats a raspberry macaroon. Mistigri is eating Brie cheese.

Soudain, ils entendent des pleurs. Une fille est assise sur un banc.

Suddenly, they hear crying. A girl is sitting on a bench.

Jules s'approche. "Que se passe-t-il ?", demande-t-il.

Jules approaches. "What's going on?", he asks.

La fille lève les yeux. "J'ai perdu mon carnet de croquis," dit-elle. "Tous mes dessins sont là."

The girl looks up. "I've lost my sketchbook," she says. "All my drawings are there."

"Ne t'inquiète pas," dit Jules. "Nous allons t'aider. Comment t'appelles-tu ?".

"Don't worry," said Jules. "We will help you. What's your name?".

"Je m'appelle Marie," répond la fille.

"My name is Marie," replies the girl.

Jules et Mistigri cherchent le carnet. Ils regardent partout

dans le musée.

Jules and Mistigri search for the notebook. They look everywhere in the museum.

Ils passent devant la Joconde. Ils voient la Vénus de Milo. Mais pas de carnet.

They pass in front of the Mona Lisa. They see the Venus de Milo. But no notebook.

Dans la galerie égyptienne, Mistigri voit quelque chose. "Jules, regarde !", dit-il doucement.

In the Egyptian gallery, Mistigri sees something. "Jules, look!", he says softly.

Le carnet est sous une vitrine. Il est coincé contre le mur.

The notebook is under a showcase. It's stuck against the wall.

"Comment le prendre ?", se demande Jules.

"How to take it?", wonders Jules.

Mistigri a une idée. Il se glisse sous la vitrine. Avec ses pattes, il pousse le carnet vers Jules.

Mistigri has an idea. He slips in under the showcase. With his paws, he pushes the notebook towards Jules.

Ils retournent vers Marie. Elle attend toujours sur le banc.

They return to Marie. She's still waiting on the bench.

"Regarde !", dit Jules. Il lui donne le carnet.

"Look!", says Jules. He gives her the notebook.

Marie est très contente. "Mon carnet ! Merci beaucoup !". Elle montre ses dessins à Jules et Mistigri.

Marie is very happy. "My notebook! Thank you so much!". She shows her drawings to Jules and Mistigri.

"Tu dessines très bien," dit Jules.

"You draw very well," said Jules.

Marie sourit : "Je veux devenir artiste."

Marie smiles: "I want to become an artist."

"Continue à dessiner," encourage Jules. "Tu réussiras."

"Keep drawing," encourages Jules. "You'll succeed."

Le soir arrive. Jules et Mistigri quittent le Louvre. Ils vont au Café Marly. De là, ils voient la pyramide du Louvre.

The evening arrives. Jules and Mistigri leave the Louvre. They go to the Café Marly. From there, they see the Louvre pyramid.

Jules mange une tarte aux pommes. Mistigri boit de la crème fraîche.

Jules eats an apple tart. Mistigri drinks fresh cream.

"Tu crois que la Joconde nous a vus ?", demande Jules.

"Do you believe that the Mona Lisa has seen us?", asks Jules.

"Oui," répond Mistigri. "Elle a même souri !".

"Yes," replies Mistigri. "She has even smiled!".

"Ah bon ? Je croyais qu'elle souriait toujours," rit Jules.

"That's good. I believed that she always smiled," laughs Jules.

Ils sourient. Ils sont heureux de leur bonne action. Ils profitent de la magie de Paris.

They smile. They're happy with their good deed. They take advantage of the magic of Paris.

Chapter 10

"Just Another Parisian Day" // "Juste une autre journée parisienne"

Photo of Camembert cheese by Uliana Dementieva.

Featured Vocabulary

The following vocabulary are presented in order of appearance...

se promènent: are taking a stroll

Jardin des Tuileries: Tuileries Garden

il fait beau: the weather is nice

le soleil: the sun

les fleurs sont: the flowers are

il regarde: he is looking at

une carte: a map

il a l'air: he has the air

s'approche de lui: approaches him

besoin d'aide: need help

s'il vous plaît: please

je cherche: I'm looking for

le musée du Louvre: the Louvre Museum

nous pouvons: we can

tout près: closeby

d'ici: from here

et voici: and here is

ils marchent: they walk

son voyage: his trip

première: first

j'ai vu: I've seen

hier: yesterday

cuisine française: French cuisine

j'ai mangé: I've eaten

en chemin: along the way

devant: in front of

artistes: artists

une jeune fille: a young girl

elle s'appelle: her name is

elle fait: she is doing

un sondage: a survey

quelle est votre: what is your

spécialité française: French specialty

j'adore: I love

le coq: the rooster

vin: wine

il pense: he's thinking

vos réponses: your responses

au Louvre: at the Louvre

impressionné par: impressed by

incroyable: incredible

pour votre aide: for your help

de rien: you're welcome

plus tard: later

dans la soirée: in the evening

sont au: are at the

boit du lait: drinks milk

on a aidé: we have helped

gastronomie française: French gastronomy

ils vont créer: they will create

un nouveau plat: a new dish

peut-être: maybe

camembert fondu: melted Camembert

est vraiment: is really

d'ailleurs: in fact

comme: as

toujours: always

Short Story: "Just Another Parisian Day"

Jules et Mistigri se promènent au Jardin des Tuileries. Il fait beau. Le soleil brille. Les fleurs sont magnifiques.

Jules and Mistigri are taking a stroll at the Tuileries Garden. The weather is nice. The sun is shining. The flowers are beautiful.

Ils voient un jeune homme. Il regarde une carte. Il a l'air perdu. Jules s'approche de lui.

They see a young man. He is looking at a map. He seems lost. Jules approaches him.

"Bonjour, vous avez besoin d'aide ?", demande Jules.

"Hello, do you need help?", asks Jules.

"Oui, s'il vous plaît," répond le jeune homme. "Je m'appelle Pierre. Je cherche le musée du Louvre."

"Yes, please," replies the young man. "My name is Pierre. I'm looking for the Louvre Museum."

"Nous pouvons vous y conduire," dit Jules. "C'est tout près d'ici. Je m'appelle Jules, et voici Mistigri."

"We can lead you there," says Jules. "It's closeby from here. My name is Jules, and here is Mistigri."

Ils marchent ensemble. Pierre parle de son voyage à Paris. C'est sa première visite.

They walk together. Pierre talks about his trip to Paris. It's his first visit.

"Paris est magnifique," dit Pierre. "J'ai vu la Tour Eiffel hier."

"Paris is beautiful," says Pierre. "I've seen the Eiffel Tower yesterday."

"Vous aimez la cuisine française ?", demande Jules.

"Do you like French cuisine?", asks Jules.

"Oh oui ! J'ai mangé des escargots. C'était délicieux !".

"Oh, yes! I've eaten snails. It was delicious!".

En chemin, ils passent devant une fontaine. Des enfants jouent. Des artistes peignent.

Along the way, they pass in front of a fountain. Children are playing. Artists are painting.

Ils rencontrent une jeune fille. Elle s'appelle Marie. Elle fait un sondage sur la cuisine française.

They meet a young girl. Her name is Marie. She is doing a survey on French cuisine.

"Quelle est votre spécialité française préférée ?", demande Marie.

"What is your favorite French specialty?", asks Marie.

"J'adore la ratatouille," répond Pierre.

"I love ratatouille," replies Pierre.

"Moi, c'est le coq au vin," dit Jules.

"For me, it's the rooster with wine," says Jules.

Mistigri miaule. Il pense au camembert.

Mistigri meows. He's thinking about Camembert.

Marie rit. "Merci pour vos réponses !".

Marie laughs. "Thank you for your responses!".

Ils arrivent au Louvre. Pierre est impressionné par la pyramide.

They arrive at the Louvre. Pierre is impressed by the pyramid.

"C'est incroyable !", s'exclame Pierre. "Merci beaucoup pour votre aide."

"It's incredible!", exclaims Pierre. "Thank you so much for your help."

"De rien," répond Jules. "Profitez bien de votre visite !".

"You're welcome," replies Jules. "Enjoy your visit!".

Plus tard dans la soirée, Jules et Mistigri sont au café. Jules mange une quiche lorraine. Mistigri boit du lait.

Later in the evening, Jules and Mistigri are at the café. Jules eats a Quiche Lorraine. Mistigri drinks milk.

"C'était une bonne journée," dit Jules. "On a aidé un touriste."

"It was a good day," says Jules. "We've helped a tourist."

"Oui," répond Mistigri. "On a même fait un sondage sur la gastronomie française."

"Yes," replies Mistigri. "We've even done a survey on French gastronomy."

"Tu crois qu'ils vont créer un nouveau plat ?", demande Jules en riant.

"Do you believe that they'll create a new dish?", asks Jules, laughing.

"Peut-être un 'ratatouille au coq au vin' !", plaisante Mistigri. "Avec du camembert fondu !".

"Maybe a 'ratatouille with rooster with wine'!", jokes Mistigri. "With melted Camembert!".

Ils rient ensemble. Paris est vraiment une ville magique. D'ailleurs, comme toujours.

They laugh together. Paris really is a magical city. In fact, as always.

Chapter 11

"Montmartre Memories" //
"Souvenirs de Montmartre"

Photo of Place du Tertre by Erwin Wodicka.

Featured Vocabulary

The following vocabulary are presented in order of appearance...

ils montent: they climb

les escaliers: the stairs

beaucoup de: a lot of

l'église: the church

une jeune femme: a young woman

un appareil photo: a camera

excusez-moi: excuse me

je veux acheter: I want to buy

un tableau souvenir: a souvenir (canvas) painting

c'est gentil: that's kind

je suis: I am

une semaine: a week

cette ville: this city

ils décident: they decide

elle hésite: she hesitates

entre: between

laquelle: which one

demande-t-elle: she asks

attentivement: closely

celle avec: the one with

très belle: very beautiful

dit-il: he says

soupe à l'oignon: onion soup

steak-frites: steak and fries

et pour: and for

le serveur: the (male) server

une assiette de: a plate of

légumes: vegetables

un café gourmand: an espresso with an assortment of tiny desserts

une boule de: a scoop of

glace à la vanille: vanilla ice cream

rentrent chez eux: return home

mais: but

dans sa chambre: in her room

chaque: each

elle pensera: she will think

le quartier: the neighborhood

vent fou: crazy wind

chats héroïques: heroic cats

en riant: laughing

Short Story: "Montmartre Memories"

Jules et Mistigri visitent Montmartre. Ils montent les escaliers vers le Sacré-Cœur. Il y a beaucoup de touristes.

Jules and Mistigri are visiting Montmartre. They climb the stairs towards the Sacré-Coeur. There are a lot of tourists.

Devant l'église, ils voient une jeune femme. Elle a un appareil photo.

In front of the church, they see a young woman. She has a camera.

"Excusez-moi," dit la jeune femme. "Je veux acheter un tableau souvenir. Vous pouvez m'aider ?".

"Excuse me," says the young woman. "I want to buy a souvenir painting. Can you help me?".

"Bien sûr," répond Jules.

"Of course," replies Jules.

La jeune femme s'appelle Amélie.

The young woman's name is Amélie.

"Merci beaucoup," dit Amélie. "C'est gentil à vous."

"Thank you very much," says Amélie. "That's kind of you."

"De rien," répond Jules. "Vous visitez Paris ?".

"You're welcome," replies Jules. "Are you visiting Paris?".

"Oui, je suis ici pour une semaine," dit Amélie. "J'adore cette ville."

"Yes, I'm here for a week," says Amélie. "I love this city."

Ils décident de visiter Montmartre ensemble. Ils voient la Place du Tertre. Des artistes peignent partout.

They decide to visit Montmartre together. They see the Place du Tertre. Artists are painting everywhere.

Amélie veut acheter un tableau. Elle hésite entre deux tableaux.

Amélie wants to buy a painting. She hesitates between two paintings.

"Laquelle préférez-vous ?", demande-t-elle à Jules.

"Which one do you prefer?", she asks to Jules.

Jules regarde attentivement. "Celle avec la Tour Eiffel est très belle," dit-il.

Jules looks closely. "The one with the Eiffel Tower is very beautiful," he says.

Amélie achète le tableau. Elle est contente de son choix.

Amélie buys the painting. She's happy with her choice.

Ils continuent leur promenade. Ils passent devant le Moulin Rouge.

They continue their stroll. They pass in front of the Moulin Rouge.

Ils arrivent au restaurant La Bonne Franquette. Amélie commande une soupe à l'oignon. Jules choisit un steak-frites.

They arrive at the restaurant, La Bonne Franquette. Amélie orders an onion soup. Jules chooses a steak and fries.

"Et pour le chat ?", demande le serveur.

"And for the cat?", asks the server.

"Une assiette de ratatouille, s'il vous plaît," dit Jules. Mistigri aime les légumes.

"A plate of ratatouille, please," says Jules. Mistigri loves vegetables.

Au dessert, Amélie prend une tarte Tatin. Jules choisit un café gourmand. Mistigri a une boule de glace à la vanille.

For dessert, Amélie takes a Tarte Tatin. Jules chooses an espresso with an assortment of tiny desserts. Mistigri has a scoop of vanilla ice cream.

Le soir, Jules et Mistigri rentrent chez eux. Ils sont fatigués mais contents.

In the evening, Jules and Mistigri return home. They are tired but happy.

"Tu crois que Amélie va accrocher son tableau dans sa chambre ?", demande Jules.

"Do you believe that Amélie will hang her painting in her room?", asks Jules.

"Donc, oui, elle va probablement l'accrocher. Et chaque fois qu'elle le regarde, elle pensera: 'Ah, Montmartre ! Le quartier des artistes, du vent fou et... des chats héroïques qui aiment la ratatouille.'", dit Mistigri en riant.

"So, yes, she'll probably hang it. And each time that she looks at it, she'll think: 'Ah, Montmartre! The neighborhood of artists, crazy wind, and... heroic cats who love ratatouille.'", says Mistigri, laughing.

Ils rient ensemble. Montmartre est vraiment un quartier magique.

They laugh together. Montmartre really is a magical neighborhood.

Chapter 12

"A Date with Mrs. Martin" // "Un rendez-vous avec Madame Martin"

Photo of a Croque Monsieur by David Pimborough.

Featured Vocabulary

The following vocabulary are presented in order of appearance...

les tableaux de: the (canvas) paintings of

monde: people

un cri: a cry

une vieille dame: an old lady

ses lunettes: her glasses

ne voit rien: can't see anything

la dame: the lady

par terre: on the floor

mon petit: my little one

beaucoup d'histoires: lots of stories

les peintres: the painters

il aimait peindre: he loved to paint

fasciné: fascinated

il apprend: he learns

choses: things

à midi: at noon

café du musée: museum café

à la sortie de: at the end of

est décoré: is decorated

faits avec: made with

produits de saison: seasonal produce

un peu de: a little bit of

fromage Manchego: Manchego cheese

après: after

un plaisir: a pleasure

qu'on: that we

trouvée: found

il y a longtemps: a long time ago

n'a toujours pas: still haven't

vrai: true

de le faire: to do it

la nuit: the night

une ville magique: a magical city

Short Story: "A Date with Mrs. Martin"

Jules et Mistigri visitent le Musée d'Orsay. Ils admirent les tableaux de Vincent van Gogh. Il y a beaucoup de monde.

Jules and Mistigri visit the Musée d'Orsay. They admire the paintings of Vincent van Gogh. There are a lot of people.

Soudain, ils entendent un cri. Une vieille dame a fait tomber ses lunettes. Elle ne voit rien sans elles.

Suddenly, they hear a cry. An old lady has dropped her glasses. She can't see anything without them.

Jules s'approche. "Je peux vous aider, madame ?", demande-t-il.

Jules approaches. "Can I help you, ma'am?", he asks.

"Oh, oui, s'il vous plaît," répond la dame. "Je ne trouve pas mes lunettes."

"Oh, yes, please," replies the lady. "I can't find my glasses."

Jules cherche par terre. Il voit les lunettes sous un banc. Il les ramasse doucement.

Jules searches on the floor. He sees the glasses under a bench. He picks them up gently.

"Voilà vos lunettes, madame," dit Jules. Il les donne à la dame.

"Here are your glasses, ma'am," says Jules. He gives them to the lady.

"Merci beaucoup, mon petit," dit la dame. "Tu es très gentil."

"Thank you very much, my little one," says the lady. "You're very kind."

La dame s'appelle Madame Martin. Elle aime beaucoup l'art. Jules et Mistigri décident de l'accompagner.

The lady's name is Mrs. Martin. She loves art very much. Jules and Mistigri decide to accompany her.

Ils regardent les tableaux ensemble. Madame Martin connaît beaucoup d'histoires sur les peintres.

They look at the paintings together. Mrs. Martin knows lots of stories about the painters.

"Regardez ce Monet," dit-elle. "Il aimait peindre son jardin à

Giverny."

"Look at this Monet," she says. "He loved to paint his garden in Giverny."

Jules est fasciné. Il apprend beaucoup de choses.

Jules is fascinated. He learns a lot of things.

À midi, ils vont au café du musée, Le Café Campana, qui se trouve à la sortie de la Galerie Impressionniste. Le café est décoré dans un style inspiré de l'Art nouveau et propose des plats faits avec des produits de saison.

At noon, they go to the museum café, Le Café Campana, which is located at the end of the Impressionist Gallery. The café is decorated in a style inspired by Art Nouveau and offers dishes made with seasonal produce.

Jules commande un croque-monsieur.

Jules orders a Croque Monsieur.

Madame Martin prend une quiche lorraine.

Madame Martin takes a Quiche Lorraine.

Mistigri reçoit un peu de fromage Manchego. Il est content.

Mistigri receives a little bit of Manchego cheese. He is delighted.

Après le repas, Madame Martin doit partir. "Merci pour cette belle visite," dit-elle.

After the meal, Mrs. Martin must leave. "Thank you for this lovely visit," she says.

"C'était un plaisir," répond Jules. "Bonne journée, Madame Martin !".

"It was a pleasure," replies Jules. "Have a nice day, Mrs. Martin!".

Le soir, Jules et Mistigri rentrent chez eux. Ils sont fatigués mais satisfaits.

In the evening, Jules and Mistigri return home. They are tired but satisfied.

"C'était une bonne journée," dit Jules. "On a aidé Madame Martin."

"It was a good day," says Jules. "We have helped Mrs. Martin."

"Oui," répond Mistigri. "Et on a appris beaucoup sur l'art."

"Yes," replies Mistigri. "And we have learned a lot about art."

Soudain, Jules se souvient de quelque chose. "Oh ! J'avais oublié la lettre pour le plus gentil !".

Suddenly, Jules remembers something. "Oh! I had forgotten the letter for the kindest!".

"Quelle lettre ?", demande Mistigri.

"What letter?", asks Mistigri.

"Tu sais, la lettre qu'on a trouvée il y a longtemps," explique Jules. "On n'a toujours pas trouvé à qui la donner."

"You know, the letter that we have found a long time ago," Jules explains. "We still haven't found who to give it to."

"C'est vrai," dit Mistigri. "Mais nous aurons encore le temps de le faire."

"That's true," says Mistigri. "But we will still have time to do it."

Ils regardent par la fenêtre. Paris brille dans la nuit. C'est vraiment une ville magique.

They look out the window. Paris sparkles in the night. It's really a magical city.

Chapter 13

"The Lucky Server" // "Le serveur chanceux"

Photo of the Palais Garnier by Anastasija Jarmolowicz.

Featured Vocabulary

The following vocabulary are presented in order of appearance...

un célèbre café: a famous café

un chocolat chaud: a hot chocolate

un peu froid: a little cold

dehors: outdoors

avant: before

un grand opéra: a big opera house

ils regardent: they look at

la belle façade: the beautiful frontage

sculptures dorées: golden sculptures

escalier en marbre: marble staircase

au plafond: on the ceiling

lustres: chandeliers

tellement: so much

je cherche du travail: I'm looking for work

est serveur: is a (male) server

un emploi: a job

bruit en cuisine: noise in the kitchen

le patron du café: the café owner

l'air inquiet: looking worried

est malade: is sick

le service du midi: (the) lunch service

peut-être: perhaps

pouvez aider: can help

à travailler: to work

les clients: the customers

le déjeuner: (the) lunch

saumon: salmon

à la fin: at the end

voulez-vous: do you want

le meilleur: the best

j'espère: I hope

n'oubliera pas: won't forget

pleine d'opportunités: full of opportunities

Short Story: "The Lucky Server"

Jules et Mistigri vont au Café de Flore. C'est un célèbre café à Paris. Ils veulent boire un chocolat chaud. Il fait un peu froid dehors.

Jules and Mistigri go to Café de Flore. It's a famous café in Paris. They want to drink a hot chocolate. It's a little cold outdoors.

Avant le café, Jules et Mistigri vont au Palais Garnier. C'est un grand opéra.

Before the café, Jules and Mistigri go to the Palais Garnier. It's a big opera house.

Ils regardent la belle façade. Il y a des sculptures dorées.

They look at the beautiful frontage. There are golden sculptures.

Ils entrent dans le hall. Ils voient un grand escalier en marbre. Il y a des peintures au plafond. Mistigri aime beaucoup les

grands lustres brillants.

They enter into the hall. They see a big marble staircase. There are paintings on the ceiling. Mistigri likes the big, brilliant chandeliers very much.

Au Café de Flore, ils voient Pierre. C'est le touriste qu'ils ont aidé au Louvre.

At the Café de Flore, they see Pierre. He's the tourist that they have helped at the Louvre.

"Bonjour Pierre !", dit Jules. "Vous êtes encore à Paris ?".

"Hello, Pierre!", says Jules. "You are still in Paris?".

"Oui," répond Pierre. "J'aime tellement cette ville. Je cherche du travail ici."

"Yes," replies Pierre. "I love this city so much. I'm searching for work here."

Pierre dit qu'il est serveur et cherche un emploi dans un café.

Pierre says that he is a server and is searching for a job in a café.

Soudain, ils entendent du bruit en cuisine. Le patron du café sort, l'air inquiet.

Suddenly, they hear noise in the kitchen. The café owner comes out, looking worried.

"Que se passe-t-il ?", demande Jules.

"What is happening?", asks Jules.

"Mon serveur est malade," répond le patron. "Je suis seul pour le service du midi."

"My server is sick," replies the owner. "I am alone for lunch service."

Jules a une idée. "Pierre est serveur," dit-il. "Il peut peut-être vous aider ?".

Jules has an idea. "Pierre is a server," he says. "He can perhaps help you?".

Le patron regarde Pierre. "C'est vrai ? Vous pouvez aider ?".

The owner looks at Pierre. "Is this true? You can help?".

"Bien sûr !", dit Pierre. Il est très heureux.

"Of course!", says Pierre. He is very happy.

Pierre commence à travailler. Il est rapide et souriant. Les clients sont satisfaits.

Pierre begins to work. He is quick and pleasant. The customers are satisfied.

Jules et Mistigri restent pour le déjeuner. Jules mange un croque-madame. Mistigri a un peu de saumon. Ils boivent aussi leur chocolat chaud.

Jules and Mistigri stay for lunch. Jules eats a Croque Madame. Mistigri has a bit of salmon. They also drink their hot chocolate.

À la fin du service, le patron est très satisfait. "Pierre, voulez-vous un emploi ici ?". Pierre accepte, heureux.

At the end of the service, the owner is very satisfied. "Pierre, do you want a job here?". Pierre happily accepts.

Jules et Mistigri rentrent chez eux le soir.

Jules and Mistigri return home in the evening.

"Tu crois qu'il va devenir le meilleur serveur de Paris ?", demande Jules en riant.

"Do you believe that he will become the best server in Paris?", asks Jules, laughing.

"Peut-être," dit Mistigri. "Mais j'espère qu'il n'oubliera pas de me donner du saumon !".

"Perhaps," says Mistigri. "But I hope that he won't forget to give me salmon!".

Ils rient ensemble. Paris est une ville pleine d'opportunités et de surprises.

They laugh together. Paris is a city full of opportunities and surprises.

Chapter 14

"What Is Kindness?" //
"Qu'est-ce que la gentillesse ?"

Photo of Grand Mosque of Paris by Elena Skalovskaia.

Featured Vocabulary

The following vocabulary are presented in order of appearance...

une belle journée d'été: a beautiful summer day

le long de la: along the

à personne: to anyone

cherchons: let's search for

le bâtiment: the building

magnifique: magnificent

motifs géométriques colorés: colorful geometric patterns

un grand chêne: a large oak tree

ce monsieur: this gentleman

si gentil: so kind

hoche la tête: nods his head

allons: let's go

l'arbre: the tree

il le fait tomber: he drops it

les mains: the hands

il donne: he gives

ravis: delighted

n'est pas finie: is not over

quelques minutes: a few minutes

le Salon de Thé: the Tea Room

de la: of the

le charmant patio: the charming patio

entourés de: surrounded by

thé à la menthe: mint tea

au miel: with honey

aux pistaches: with pistachios

une petite assiette: a small plate

loukoums à la rose: rose-flavored Turkish delights

une seule personne: just one person

tous ces gens: all these people

chaque jour: each day

tu as raison: you're right

partout à Paris: everywhere in Paris

Short Story: "What Is Kindness?"

Par une belle journée d'été, Jules et Mistigri se promènent le long de la Seine. Soudain, Jules s'arrête.

On a beautiful summer day, Jules and Mistigri are strolling along the Seine. Suddenly, Jules stops.

"Mistigri, tu te souviens de la lettre pour le plus gentil ? Nous ne l'avons toujours donné à personne !".

"Mistigri, do you remember the letter for the kindest? We still haven't given it to anyone!".

"C'est vrai," répond Mistigri. "Cherchons le plus gentil de Paris aujourd'hui."

"That's true," replies Mistigri. "Let's search for the kindest in Paris today."

Ils continuent leur promenade et arrivent au Grand Mosquée de Paris. Le bâtiment est magnifique avec des motifs

géométriques colorés.

They continue their stroll and arrive at the Grand Mosque of Paris. The building is magnificent with colorful geometric patterns.

Ils voient un vieil homme aider un petit garçon. Le ballon du garçon est coincée dans un grand chêne. Le vieil homme se débat.

They see an old man helping a little boy. The boy's ball is stuck in a large oak tree. The old man is struggling.

"Regarde, Jules," dit Mistigri. "Ce monsieur est si gentil d'essayer d'aider."

"Look, Jules," says Mistigri. "This gentleman is so kind to try to help."

Jules hoche la tête. "Oui, allons l'aider à aider."

Jules nods his head. "Yes, let's go help him to help."

Ils s'approchent discrètement. Jules grimpe rapidement à l'arbre et attrape le ballon. Il le fait tomber doucement dans les mains du vieil homme.

They approach discreetly. Jules quickly climbs the tree and grabs the ball. He drops it gently into the hands of the old man.

Le vieil homme est surpris. "Oh, mais comment... ?".

The old man is surprised. "Oh, but how...?".

Il donne le ballon au petit garçon qui sourit de joie. "Merci beaucoup, monsieur !".

He hands the ball to the little boy, who smiles with joy. "Thank you very much, sir!".

Jules et Mistigri observent la scène, ravis.

Jules and Mistigri observe the scene, delighted.

"C'était vraiment gentil," dit Jules. "Peut-être que c'est lui le plus gentil de Paris ?".

"That was truly kind," says Jules. "Maybe it's him that is the kindest in Paris?".

"Peut-être," répond Mistigri. "Mais la journée n'est pas finie."

"Maybe," replies Mistigri. "But the day is not over."

Quelques minutes plus tard, ils voient une jeune fille aider une dame âgée à monter les escaliers.

A few minutes later, they see a young girl helping an elderly lady to climb the stairs.

"Encore un acte de gentillesse," remarque Mistigri.

"Another act of kindness," remarks Mistigri.

Jules acquiesce. "Paris est pleine de gens gentils."

Jules nods. "Paris is full of kind people."

Ils se dirigent à côté vers le Salon de Thé de la Grande Mosquée de Paris.

They head next door to the Tea Room of the Grand Mosque of Paris.

Ils s'assoient dans le charmant patio, entourés de mosaïques colorées et de plantes verdoyantes. Jules commande un thé à la menthe et des baklavas au miel et aux pistaches. Mistigri déguste une petite assiette de loukoums à la rose.

They sit in the charming patio, surrounded by colorful mosaics and verdant plants. Jules orders a mint tea and baklava with honey and pistachios. Mistigri savors a small plate of rose-flavored Turkish delights.

"Alors, à qui devons-nous donner la lettre ?", demande Jules.

"So, to whom should we give the letter ?", asks Jules.

Mistigri réfléchit. "Tu sais, Jules, peut-être que le plus gentil

n'est pas une seule personne. Peut-être que c'est tous ces gens qui font de petits gestes gentils chaque jour."

Mistigri thinks. "You know, Jules, maybe the kindest isn't just one person. Maybe it's all these people who do little, kind gestures each day."

Jules sourit. "Tu as raison, Mistigri. La gentillesse est partout à Paris."

Jules smiles. "You're right, Mistigri. Kindness is everywhere in Paris."

Chapter 15

"An Improvised Concert" // "Un concert improvisé"

Photo from the Champ de Mars by Sergii Kolesnyk.

Featured Vocabulary

The following vocabulary are presented in order of appearance...

le long: along

près d'eux: near them

il tient: he is holding

une guitare: a guitar

le père de Sophie: Sophie's father

pourquoi êtes-vous: why are you

je dois: I must

jouer de la musique: play music

ma voix: my voice

je ne peux pas: I can't

chanter: sing

à cause: because of

un rhume: a cold

j'ai besoin d'argent: I need money

mes chansons: my songs

je peux apprendre: I can learn

amusé: amused

vous seriez: you would be

à jouer de la guitare: to play the guitar

attentivement: carefully

la mesure: the measure

avec sa queue: with his tail

bientôt: soon

est douce: is soft

en rythme: in rhythm

s'arrêtent pour écouter: stop to listen

la musique: the music

elle est surprise: she is surprised

avec son père: with her father

incroyable: incredible

après une heure: after an hour

beaucoup de monde: a lot of people

le chapeau de Thomas: Thomas' hat

amusant: fun

juste en face du parc: right in front of the park

tu as découvert: you have discovered

un nouveau talent: a new talent

tu crois que: do you think that

une star de la chanson: a singing star

ton choriste félin: your feline backup vocalist

dans leurs oreilles: in their ears

surprises musicales: musical surprises

Short Story: "An Improvised Concert"

Jules et Mistigri se promènent le long du Champ de Mars. Il fait beau. La Tour Eiffel brille au soleil. Des enfants jouent au ballon près d'eux.

Jules and Mistigri are taking a stroll along the Champ de Mars. The weather is nice. The Eiffel Tower gleams in the sun. Children are playing ball near them.

Ils voient un jeune homme triste. Il tient une guitare. C'est Thomas, le père de Sophie. Il est assis sur un banc.

They see a sad young man. He is holding a guitar. It's Thomas, Sophie's father. He's sitting on a bench.

"Bonjour Thomas," dit Jules. "Pourquoi êtes-vous triste ?".

"Hello, Thomas," says Jules. "Why are you sad?".

"Je dois jouer de la musique ici," répond Thomas. "Mais j'ai perdu ma voix. Je ne peux pas chanter."

"I must play music here," Thomas replies. "But I've lost my voice. I can't sing."

"C'est à cause du froid ?", demande Mistigri.

"Is it because of the cold?", asks Mistigri.

"Oui, j'ai attrapé un rhume hier," explique Thomas. "C'est terrible, mais j'ai besoin d'argent."

"Yes, I've caught a cold yesterday," explains Thomas. "It's terrible, but I need money."

**Jules réfléchit. Il a une idée. "Je peux chanter pour vous,"
propose-t-il.**

Jules thinks. He has an idea. "I can sing for you," he proposes.

Thomas est surpris. "Vraiment ? Tu connais mes chansons ?".

Thomas is surprised. "Really? You know my songs?".

**"Non, mais je peux apprendre," dit Jules. "Mistigri peut
m'aider."**

"No, but I can learn," says Jules. "Mistigri can help me."

"Comment un chat peut-il aider ?", demande Thomas, amusé.

"How can a cat help?", asks Thomas, amused.

"Vous seriez surpris," répond Jules en souriant.

"You would be surprised," replies Jules with a smile.

**Thomas sourit aussi. Il commence à jouer de la guitare. Jules
écoute attentivement. Mistigri bat la mesure avec sa queue.**

Thomas smiles too. He begins to play the guitar. Jules listens
carefully. Mistigri beats the measure with his tail.

**Bientôt, Jules commence à chanter. Sa voix est douce. Mistigri
miaule en rythme.**

Soon, Jules begins to sing. His voice is soft. Mistigri meows in rhythm.

Les gens s'arrêtent pour écouter. Ils aiment la musique. Certains dansent.

People stop to listen. They like the music. Some dance.

Sophie arrive. Elle est surprise de voir Jules chanter avec son père.

Sophie arrives. She is surprised to see Jules singing with her father.

"C'est incroyable !", dit-elle. "Vous formez un super duo !".

"It's incredible!", she says. "You make a great duo!".

"Jules nous sauve la journée," explique Thomas à sa fille.

"Jules saves the day for us," explains Thomas to his daughter.

Après une heure, il y a beaucoup de monde. Ils applaudissent avec enthousiasme. Certains mettent de l'argent dans le chapeau de Thomas.

After an hour, there are a lot of people. They applaud with enthusiasm. Some put money in Thomas's hat.

Thomas est très content. "Merci Jules," dit-il. "Tu as sauvé mon concert."

Thomas is very happy. "Thank you, Jules," he says. "You have saved my concert."

"De rien," répond Jules. "C'était amusant."

"You're welcome," replies Jules. "It was fun."

Ce soir-là, Jules et Mistigri mangent des crêpes au Nutella au Bistrot Le Champ de Mars. C'est un charmant bistro juste en face du parc. Ils sont fatigués mais heureux.

That evening, Jules and Mistigri eat Nutella crepes at the Bistrot Le Champ de Mars. It's a charming bistro right in front of the park. They are tired but happy.

"C'était une belle journée," dit Jules. "On a aidé Thomas."

"It was a beautiful day," says Jules. "We have helped Thomas."

"Oui," répond Mistigri. "Et tu as découvert un nouveau talent."

"Yes," replies Mistigri. "And you've discovered a new talent."

"Tu crois que je peux devenir une star de la chanson ?", demande Jules en riant.

"Do you think that I can become a singing star?", asks Jules, laughing.

"Peut-être," dit Mistigri. "Mais n'oublie pas ton choriste félin !".

"Perhaps," says Mistigri. "But don't forget your feline backup vocalist!".

Ils rient ensemble. La musique résonne encore dans leurs oreilles. Paris est vraiment une ville pleine de surprises musicales.

They laugh together. The music still resonates in their ears. Paris is truly a city full of musical surprises.

Chapter 16

"Mistigri's Secret" // "Le secret de Mistigri"

Photo of Jardin des Plantes by Tromp Willem Van Urk.

Featured Vocabulary

The following vocabulary are presented in order of appearance...

un beau jardin: a beautiful garden

beaucoup de fleurs: lots of flowers

arbres: trees

le labyrinthe des plantes: the maze of plants

dans l'espoir de: in the hope of

animaux plus rares: rarer animals

qui cherche: who is looking for

petit chat en peluche: small stuffed cat

appelle-t-elle: she calls

gentiment: gently

on va t'aider: we will help you

à le retrouver: to find it

sous les bancs: under the benches

dans les buissons: in the bushes

de là-haut: from up there

mieux: better

quelque chose de blanc: something white

là-bas: over there

vers l'endroit: towards the place

on a trouvé: we've found

très contente: very glad

avec un grand sourire: with a big smile

la maman de Léa: Lea's mom

cette aventure: this adventure

une tarte aux pommes: an apple tart

un bol de lait: a bowl of milk

le soir: (in) the evening

il semble: he seems

avec un petit sourire: with a small smile

en fait: actually

je sais depuis longtemps: I've known for a long time

le destinataire: the recipient

avant: before

je l'ai gardé: I've kept it

je pense que: I think that

dans la nuit: in the night

une ville magique: a magical city

gens gentils: kind people

et vous: and you

lecteurs: readers

avez-vous deviné: have you guessed

Short Story: "Mistigri's Secret"

Jules et Mistigri vont au Jardin des Plantes. C'est un beau jardin à Paris. Il y a beaucoup de fleurs et d'arbres. Ils se promènent dans le labyrinthe des plantes.

Jules and Mistigri go to the Jardin des Plantes. It's a beautiful garden in Paris. There are lots of flowers and trees. They walk through the maze of plants.

Ensuite, ils se rendent dans un zoo dans l'espoir de voir des animaux plus rares.

And then, they visit a zoo in the hope of seeing rarer animals.

Ils voient une petite fille qui cherche quelque chose. Elle s'appelle Léa. Elle a perdu son petit chat en peluche.

They see a little girl who is looking for something. Her name is Léa. She has lost her small stuffed cat.

"Minou, minou !", appelle-t-elle doucement.

"Kitty, kitty!", she calls softly.

"Tu cherches ton chat en peluche ?", demande Jules gentiment. "On va t'aider à le retrouver."

"Are you looking for your stuffed cat?", Jules asks gently. "We'll help you to find it."

Ils cherchent partout dans le jardin. Ils regardent sous les bancs. Ils cherchent dans les buissons.

They search everywhere in the garden. They look under the benches. They search in the bushes.

Mistigri a une idée. Il grimpe dans un arbre. De là-haut, il voit

mieux.

Mistigri has an idea. He climbs up a tree. From up there, he sees better.

"Jules !", appelle Mistigri. "Je vois quelque chose de blanc là-bas !".

"Jules!", calls Mistigri. "I see something white over there!".

Jules court vers l'endroit que Mistigri montre. Il trouve le petit chat en peluche.

Jules runs towards the place that Mistigri is showing. He finds the little stuffed cat.

"Regarde Léa," dit Jules. "On a trouvé ton chat !".

"Look, Léa," says Jules. "We've found your cat!".

Léa est très contente. Elle serre fort son chat en peluche. "Merci beaucoup !", dit-elle avec un grand sourire.

Léa is very glad. She hugs her stuffed cat tightly. "Thank you so much!", she says with a big smile.

La maman de Léa arrive. Elle remercie aussi Jules et Mistigri. "Vous êtes très gentils," dit-elle.

Léa's mom arrives. She also thanks Jules and Mistigri. "You're very kind," she says.

Après cette aventure, Jules et Mistigri vont au café du jardin. Jules mange une tarte aux pommes. Mistigri boit un bol de lait.

After this adventure, Jules and Mistigri go to the garden café. Jules eats an apple tart. Mistigri drinks a bowl of milk.

Ils rentrent chez eux le soir. Jules regarde la lettre pour "le plus gentil".

They return home in the evening. Jules looks at the letter for "the kindest".

"Je n'ai toujours pas trouvé le plus gentil de Paris," dit Jules. Il semble triste.

"I still haven't found the kindest in Paris," says Jules. He seems sad.

Mistigri le regarde avec un petit sourire. "En fait, je sais depuis longtemps qui est le destinataire de cette lettre."

Mistigri looks at him with a small smile. "Actually, I've known for a long time who the recipient of this letter is."

Jules est très surpris. "Vraiment ? Qui est-ce ? Et pourquoi tu ne me l'as pas dit avant ?".

Jules is very surprised. "Really? Who's is it? And why didn't you tell me before?".

"Je l'ai gardé secret," répond Mistigri. "Mais je pense que je vais encore le garder un peu."

"I've kept it a secret," replies Mistigri. "But I think that I will keep it a little longer."

"Oh, Mistigri !", dit Jules en riant. "Tu es plein de surprises !".

"Oh, Mistigri!", says Jules, laughing. "You're full of surprises!".

Ils regardent par la fenêtre. Paris brille dans la nuit. C'est une ville magique, pleine de gens gentils.

They look out the window. Paris sparkles in the night. It's a magical city, full of kind people.

"Et vous, lecteurs," demande Mistigri, "avez-vous deviné qui est le destinataire ?".

"And you, readers," asks Mistigri, "have you guessed who the recipient is?".

French A1 Vocabulary Glossary // Glossaire de vocabulaire français A1

A

à: to, at, in

acheter: (to) buy

l'alcool: (the) alcohol, (the) fruit brandy

l'adolescent: (the) teenager

l'adulte: (the) adult

l'aéroport: (the) airport

l'âge: (the) age

âgé(e): elderly

aider: (to) help

aigre: sour

l'ail: (the) garlic

ailleurs: elsewhere

aimer: (to) love, (to) like, (to) enjoy

l'air: (the) air

l'air frais: (the) fresh air, (the) cool air

aller: (to) go

allégé(e): reduced, lightened, low-fat

l'amande: (the) almond

l'ami(e): (the) friend

l'amour: (the) love

s'amuser: (to) have fun (reflexive verb)

l'ananas: (the) pineapple

ancien(ne): old (not describing a person), former

l'animal: (the) animal

l'animal de compagnie: (the) pet

l'année: (the) year

l'année dernière: (the) last year

l'année prochaine: (the) next year

l'anniversaire: (the) birthday

l'appareil photo: (the) camera

l'appartement: (the) apartment

appeler: (to) call

après: after, following

après-demain: the day after tomorrow

l'après-midi: (the) afternoon

l'arbre: (the) tree

l'argent: (the) money, (the) silver (metal)

l'argent liquide: (the) cash

l'arrêt de bus: (the) bus stop

arrêter: (to) stop, (to) turn off

arriver: (to) arrive, (to) happen

s'asseoir: (to) sit down

l'assiette: (the) plate

l'atelier: (the) workshop, (the) artist's studio

attendre: (to) wait (for)

au revoir: goodbye

l'aubergine: (the) eggplant

aujourd'hui: today

aussi: also

autre: other

avant: before, prior to

avant-hier: the day before yesterday

avec: with

avoir: (to) have

B

(le) bain: (the) bath

(la) balle: (the) ball (small like in golf or tennis)

(le) ballon: (the) ball (large like in basketball or soccer/football)

(le) bambin: (the) toddler

(la) banane: (the) banana

(le) banc: (the) bench

(la) banque: (the) bank

bas(se): low

(le) basilic: (the) basil

(le) bateau: (the) boat

(le) bâtiment: (the) building

beau: handsome, nice (male)

beaucoup: many, much, a lot

(le) beau-fils: (the) son-in-law

(le) beau-frère: (the) brother-in-law

(le) beau-père: (the) father-in-law

(le) bébé: (the) baby

belle: beautiful, lovely (female)

(la) belle-fille: (the) daughter-in-law

(la) belle-mère: (the) mother-in-law

(la) belle-sœur: (the) sister-in-law

besoin: (to) need

(le) beurre: (the) butter

(le) beurre doux: (the) mild butter (no added salt)

(le) beurre salé: (the) salted butter

(la) bibliothèque: (the) library

bien: well, fine, good

bientôt: soon, shortly

bienvenue: welcome

(la) bière: (the) beer

biologique: organic

(le) bistrot: (the) bistro

boire: (to) drink

(la) boisson: (the) drink, (the) beverage

(la) boisson non alcoolisée: (the) non-alcoholic drink

(la) boîte: (the) can, (the) box

(la) boîte à lettres: (the) mailbox

(le) bol: (the) bowl

bon(ne): good, kind, nice

bonjour: hello, good morning, good day, good afternoon

bonne journée: have a nice day

bonne nuit: have a good night

bonne soirée: have a good evening

bonsoir: good evening, good night

(la) boulangerie: (the) bakery

(le) bœuf: (the) beef

(la) brasserie: (the) brewery

briller: (to) shine, (to) sparkle, (to) glow

(la) brise: (the) breeze

brûlé(e): burnt

bruyant(e): noisy

(le) bureau: (the) office, (the) desk

(le) bureau de poste: (the) post office

(le) bus: (the) bus

C

(le) café: (the) coffee, (the) coffee shop

(le) café au lait: (the) milk coffee

(le) café noir: (the) black coffee

(la) caisse: (the) cash register

calme: quiet, calm

(la) carotte: (the) carrot

(la) carte: (the) map, (the) card, (the) menu, (the) transportation pass

(la) carte de crédit: (the) credit card

(la) carte des vins: (the) wine list

(la) carte d'embarquement: (the) boarding pass

(la) carte d'identité: (the) identity card

(la) carte postale: (the) postcard

cassé(e): broken

(la) cave: (the) cellar

ce(tte): this, that

célèbre: famous

(le) centre commercial: (the) shopping mall

(la) cerise: (the) cherry

c'est: it is

chacun(e): each one, every one (pronoun)

(la) chaise: (the) chair

(la) chambre: (the) bedroom, (the) room

(la) chambre d'hôte: (the) bed and breakfast

(le) champ: (the) field

(le) champ de courses: (the) racecourse

(le) champignon: (the) mushroom

(la) chance: (the) luck

chaque: each, every (adjective)

(le) chat: (the) cat

(le) château: (the) castle, (the) mansion

(le) chaton: (the) kitten

chaud(e): hot, warm

cher: dear, expensive (masculine)

chère: dear, expensive (feminine)

(le) cheval: (the) horse

chez: at the house of

chez moi: at my home

(le) chien: (the) dog

(le) chiot: (the) puppy

(le) chocolat: (the) chocolate

(le) chocolat chaud: (the) hot chocolate

(le) chocolat noir: (the) dark chocolate

(le) choix: (the) choice, (the) selection

(la) chose: (the) thing

(le) ciel: (the) sky

(le) cimetière: (the) cemetary, (the) graveyard

(le) citron: (the) lemon

(le) citron vert: (the) lime

clair(e): clear, bright

(le) code postal: (the) postal code

combien: how much, how many

commander: (to) order (food, online purchase, etc.)

comme: as, like

commencer: (to) begin

comment: how

conduire: (to) drive

(la) confiture: (the) jam

connaître: (to) know (someone)

continuer: (to) continue, (to) keep

contre: against, versus

courir: (to) run

(le) cousin: (the) cousin (male)

(la) cousine: (the) cousin (female)

(le) couteau: (the) knife

(la) crème: (the) cream

(la) crème glacée: (the) ice cream

(la) crêpe: (the) crepe

(la) crêpe salée: (the) savory crepe

(la) crêpe sucrée: (the) sweet crepe

crier: (to) shout

croire: (to) believe, (to) think

(le) croissant: (the) croissant

(le) croissant aux amandes: (the) almond croissant

(la) cuillère: (the) spoon

(la) cuisine: (the) kitchen, (the) cooking, (the) cuisine

(la) cuisine familiale: (the) home cooking

cuisiner: (to) cook

cuit(e): cooked

D

d': of, from, about (preposition for words starting with a vowel or silent "h")

(la) dame: (the) lady

dans: in, into

(la) date: (the) date (day)

(la) date de naissance: (the) date of birth

de: from, of, some

de rien: you're welcome (informal)

décaféiné(e): decaffeinated

dedans: inside

dehors: outside

(le) déjeuner: (the) lunch

délicieuse: delicious (feminine)

délicieux: delicious (masculine)

demain: tomorrow

demander: (to) ask

désolé(e): sorry

devant: in front (of)

devoir: (to) have to, must

difficile: difficult

(le) dîner: (the) dinner

dire: (to) say, (to) tell

disparu(e): missing, disappeared (person)

dormir: (to) sleep

douce: sweet, soft, mild (feminine)

(la) douche: (the) shower

(se) doucher: (to) take a shower (reflexive verb)

doux: sweet, soft, mild (masculine)

droite: right (spatial direction)

E

l'eau: (the) water

l'eau gazeuse: (the) sparkling water

l'eau potable: (the) drinking water

l'école: (the) school

écouter: (to) listen to

écrire: (to) write

elle: she, it (feminine pronoun)

elles: they (feminine only pronoun)

en: to, in, at

en bas: below, downstairs

en haut: above, upstairs

encore: still, yet, again

s'endormir: (to) fall asleep (reflexive verb)

énergique: energetic

l'enfant: (the) child

ensemble: together

ensoleillé(e): sunny

entendre: (to) hear

entre: between

l'épice: (the) spice

l'épicerie: (the) groceries, (the) grocery store

l'escalier: (the) staircase

et: and

l'étoile: (the) star (in the sky)

être: (to) be

excusez-moi: excuse me

extraordinaire: extraordinary

F

facile: easy

faible(sse): weak

faire: (to) make, (to) do

(la) famille: (the) family

(la) famille proche: (the) immediate family

fatigué(e): tired, exhausted

(la) femme: (the) woman, (the) wife

(la) fenêtre: (the) window

fermé(e): closed

fermer: (to) close, (to) turn off

(la) fête: (the) holiday, (the) party

(la) figue: (the) fig

(la) fille: (the) girl, (the) daughter

(le) fils: (the) son

fini(e): finished

finir: (to) finish, (to) end

(la) fleur: (the) flower

(la) fontaine: (the) fountain

(la) forêt: (the) forest

fort(e): strong

(la) fourchette: (the) fork

fraîche: fresh, cool (feminine)

frais: fresh, cool (masculine)

(la) fraise: (the) strawberry

(la) framboise: (the) raspberry

(le) frère: (the) brother

froid(e): cold

(le) fromage: (the) cheese

(le) fromage brie: (the) Brie cheese

(le) fromage camembert: (the) Camembert cheese

(le) fromage cheddar: (the) cheddar cheese

(le) fromage de chèvre: (the) goat cheese

(le) fromage feta: (the) feta cheese

(le) fruit: (the) fruit

(le) fruit biologique: (the) organic fruit (biologique can be shortened to bio as well)

(les) fruits de mer: (the) seafood (plural)

G

(le) garage: (the) garage

(le) garçon: (the) boy, (the) male server

(la) gare: (the) railway station

garer: (to) park

(le) gâteau: (the) cake

(le) gâteau au chocolat: (the) chocolate cake

(le) gâteau au fromage: (the) cheesecake

gauche: left (spatial direction)

gelé(e): frozen

(les) gens: (the) people, (the) folks

gentil(le): kind, nice

(la) glace: (the) ice, (the) ice cream, (the) mirror

(la) glace à la noisette: (the) hazelnut ice cream

(la) glace à la vanille: (the) vanilla ice cream

(le) glaçon: (the) ice cube

(le) goût: (the) taste, (the) flavor

grand(e): big, large, tall

(le) grand magasin: (the) department store

(la) grand-mère: (the) grandmother

(le) grand-père: (the) grandfather

gras(se): fat, greasy

(la) grenade: (the) pomegranate

(la) grotte: (the) cave

H

s'habiller: (to) get dressed (reflexive verb)

habiter: (to) live (in)

(le) haricot: (the) bean

haut(e): high, tall

(la) hauteur: (the) height

l'herbe: (the) herb, (the) grass

l'heure: (the) hour, (the) time of the day

heureuse: happy, pleased (feminine)

heureux: happy, pleased (masculine)

hier: yesterday

l'homme: (the) man

l'hôpital: (the) hospital

l'hôtel: (the) hotel

l'hôtel de ville: (the) town hall

l'huile: (the) oil

l'huile d'olive: (the) olive oil

I

ici: here

ici même: right here

idéal(e): ideal

l'idée: (the) idea

il: he, it (masculine pronoun)

il y a: there is, there are, ago

l'île: (the) island

ils: they (masculine only or mixed gender pronoun)

inclus(e): included, inclusive

l'instant: (the) moment

intéressant(e): interesting

introduire: (to) introduce, (to) insert

l'invité(e): (the) guest

l'invité(e) de la fête: (the) party guest

J

j': I (before verbs starting with a vowel or silent "h")

jamais: never

(le) jambon: (the) ham

(le) jardin: (the) garden

je: I (before verbs starting with a consonant)

je vous en prie: you're welcome (formal)

jeune: young

(la) joie: (the) joy, (the) happiness

joli(e): pretty

jouer: (to) play (games)

(le) jour: (the) calendar day

(le) jour férié: (the) public holiday

(le) journal: (the) newspaper

(la) journée: (the) daytime

joyeux anniversaire: happy birthday

(le) jus: (the) juice

(le) jus de fruit: (the) fruit juice

(le) jus d'orange: (the) orange juice

K

kascher: kosher

(le) ketchup: (the) ketchup

(le) kiosque: (the) kiosk, (the) newsstand

(le) kiwi: (the) kiwi (fruit)

(le) kumquat: (the) kumquat

L

l': the (definite article for singular nouns starting with a vowel or silent "h")

la: the (definite article for feminine nouns)

là: there

(le) lac: (the) lake

(le) lait: (the) milk

(le) lait écrémé: (the) non-fat milk

(le) lait entier: (the) whole milk

(la) laitue: (the) lettuce

(le) lapin: (the) rabbit

le: the (definite article for masculine nouns)

léger: lightweight (masculine)

légère: lightweight (feminine)

(le) légume: (the) vegetable

(le) légume de saison: (the) seasonal vegetable

les: the (definite article for plural nouns)

(la) lettre: (the) letter

(la) librairie: (the) bookshop

lire: (to) read

(le) lit: (the) bed

(le) livre: (the) book

longtemps: a long time

lourd(e): heavy, muggy

(la) lumière: (the) light

(la) lumière du soleil: (the) sunlight

(la) lune: (the) moon

(la) lunette: (the) pair of eyeglasses

(la) lunette de soleil: (the) pair of sunglasses

M

Madame: Mrs., Ms.

Mademoiselle: Miss, Ms.

(le) magasin: (the) store, (the) shop

maigre: skinny, slender

(la) main: (the) hand

maintenant: now

mais: but

(le) maïs: (the) corn

(la) maison: (the) house, (the) home

mal: badly

malade: sick

manger: (to) eat

(le) marché: (the) market, (the) marketplace

marcher: (to) walk

(le) mari: (the) husband

marié(e): married

(le) marron: (the) chestnut

(le) matin: (the) morning

mauvais(e): bad

(la) mayonnaise: (the) mayonnaise

meilleur(e): best, better (quality)

(la) menthe: (the) mint

(le) menu: (the) menu

(la) mer: (the) sea

merci: thank you

merci beaucoup: thank you very much

(la) mère: (the) mother

(le) métro: (the) metro, (the) subway

(le) midi: (the) noon, (the) midday

(le) miel: (the) honey

(la) minuit: (the) midnight

(la) minute: (the) minute

moins: less, minus

(le) mois: (the) month

(le) mois dernier: last month

(le) mois prochain: next month

(le) monde: (the) world

Monsieur: Sir, Mr.

(la) montagne: (the) mountain

(la) moule: (the) mussel (seafood)

(les) moules-frites: (the) cooked mussels with French fries

(la) moutarde: (the) mustard

(la) moutarde à l'ancienne: (the) whole grain mustard

(le) mur: (the) wall

(la) mûre: (the) blackberry

(le) musée: (the) museum

(le) musée d'art: (the) art museum

(la) myrtille: (the) blueberry

N

(la) nappe: (the) tablecloth

naturel(le): natural

(la) neige: (the) snow

neiger: (to) snow

(le) neveu: (the) nephew

(la) nièce: (the) niece

(la) noisette: (the) hazelnut

(le) nom: (the) name

(le) nom de famille: (the) family name

(le) nom de jeune fille: (the) maiden name

(le) nombre: (the) number (amount of something)

non: no, not

non alcoolisé(e): non-alcoholic

(la) nourriture: (the) food

nous: we

nouveau: new (masculine)

nouvelle: new (feminine)

(le) nuage: (the) cloud

nuageuse: cloudy (feminine)

nuageux: cloudy (masculine)

(la) nuit: (the) night

(le) numéro: (the) number (identifier like house number)

O

l'océan: (the) ocean

l'oignon: (the) onion

l'oignon caramélisé: (the) caramelized onion

l'oiseau: (the) bird

on: we (informal pronoun)

l'oncle: (the) uncle

l'or: (the) gold (metal)

l'orange: (the) orange (fruit)

ordinaire: ordinary

ou: or

où: where

l'œuf: (the) egg

l'œuf mayonnaise: (the) mayonnaise egg (mayonnaise can be shortened to mayo as well)

oui: yes

ouvert(e): open

P

(le) pain: (the) bread

(le) pain aux raisins: (the) raisin bread

(le) pain perdu: (the) French toast (common breakfast food around the world)

(le) pamplemousse: (the) grapefruit

(le) parc: (the) park

(le) parent: (the) parent, (the) relative

parler: (to) talk

partir: (to) leave

(la) patate: (the) sweet potato

(la) pâtisserie: (the) pastry, (the) pastry shop

(le) pays: (the) country

(la) pêche: (the) peach

penser: (to) think

(le) père: (the) father

(la) personne: (the) person

petit(e): small, little, short

(le) petit ami: (the) boyfriend

(la) petite amie: (the) girlfriend

(le) petit-déjeuner: (the) breakfast

(le) petit-fils: (the) grandson

(la) petite-fille: (the) granddaughter

peu: few

(la) pharmacie: (the) pharmacy

(la) plage: (the) beach

pleuvoir: (to) rain

(la) pluie: (the) rain

plus: more, plus

plus tard: later

plus tôt: earlier

(la) poire: (the) pear

(le) poisson: (the) fish

(le) poivre: (the) pepper

(la) pomme: (the) apple

(la) pomme de terre: (the) potato

(le) porc: (the) pork

porter: (to) wear

(le) poulet: (the) chicken

pour: for, in order to

pourquoi: why

pouvoir: (to) be able to, can

prendre: (to) take

(le) prénom: (the) first name, (the) given name

près: near

profiter: (to) enjoy, (to) take advantage

propre: clean, neat

(la) prune: (the) plum

Q

qu': that (subordinating conjunction before a vowel or silent "h")

quand: when

que: that (subordinating conjunction before a consonant)

quel(le): what, which (a choice between two or more options)

qui: who, whom

(la) quiche: (the) quiche

(la) quiche lorraine: (the) quiche originally from Lorraine with cheese and bacon

quoi: what (when asking question in uncertainty)

R

(le) raisin: (the) grape

rechercher: (to) search for

regarder: (to) watch, (to) look at

remercier: (to) thank

(le) repas: (the) meal

répondre: (to) reply, (to) answer

(le) restaurant: (the) restaurant

(se) réveiller: (to) wake up (reflexive verb)

(le) rhum: (the) rum (beverage)

rire: (to) laugh

(la) rivière: (the) river

(le) riz: (the) rice

rouler: (to) ride, (to) drive, (to) roll

(la) rue: (the) street

(la) rue pavée: (the) cobblestone street

S

s': himself, herself, itself, oneself, themselves (reflexive pronoun before a verb starting with a consonant)

(le) sable: (the) sand

sain(e): healthy

(la) salade: (the) salad

(la) salade niçoise: (the) salad originally from Nice with boiled eggs and anchovies or tuna

salé(e): salty, savory

(la) salle à manger: (the) dining room

(la) salle de bain: (the) bathroom

(la) salle de séjour: (the) living room

(la) salle de sport: (the) gym

salut: hi, hey, bye (informal)

(la) sauce: (the) sauce, (the) gravy

(la) sauce béchamel: (the) bechamel sauce

(la) sauce tomate: (the) tomato sauce

(le) saumon: (the) salmon

sauter: (to) jump

savoir: (to) know (something)

savourer: (to) taste, (to) savor

(le) scooter: (the) scooter

se: himself, herself, itself, oneself, themselves (reflexive pronoun before a verb starting with a vowel or silent "h")

(la) seconde: (the) second (unit of time)

(le) sel: (the) salt

(la) semaine: (the) week

(la) semaine dernière: (the) last week

(la) semaine prochaine: (the) next week

sentir: (to) smell

seul(e): alone

s'il vous plaît: please

skier: (to) ski

(la) soirée: (the) evening

(le) soleil: (the) sun

sombre(ée): dark, dim

(la) soupe: (the) soup

(la) soupe à l'oignon: (the) onion soup

(la) sœur: (the) sister

sourire: (to) smile

sous: under

(la) station de métro: (the) metro station

(le) sucre: (the) sugar

sur: on

(le) surnom: (the) nickname

T

(la) table: (the) table (furniture)

(le) tableau: (the) canvas painting, (the) chart, (the) data table

(la) tante: (the) aunt

(la) tarte: (the) tart, (the) pie

(la) tarte aux myrtilles: (the) blueberry tart

(la) tarte aux pommes: (the) apple tart

(la) tasse: (the) cup

(le) taxi: (the) taxi

(le) temps: (the) weather

(le) thé: (the) tea

(le) thé au lait: (the) tea with milk

(le) thé noir: (the) black tea

(la) toilette: (the) toilet

(la) tomate: (the) tomato

très: very

triste: sad

tu: you (informal singular)

U

ultérieur(e): subsequent, later

ultime: ultimate, final, last

un: a, an (indefinite article for masculine nouns)

un peu: a little bit

une: a, an (indefinite article for feminine nouns)

V

(la) vanille: (the) vanilla

vendre: (to) sell

venir: (to) come

(le) vent: (the) wind

venteuse: windy (feminine)

venteux: windy (masculine)

vers: to, towards

(la) viande: (the) meat

vieille: old (to describe a person, feminine)

vieux: old (to describe a person, masculine)

(la) ville: (the) city, (the) town

(le) vin: (the) wine

(le) vin blanc: (the) white wine

(le) vin rosé: (the) rosé wine

(le) vin rouge: (the) red wine

(le) vinaigre: (the) vinegar

(le) vinaigre de cidre de pomme: (the) apple cider vinegar

(le) vinaigre de vin: (the) wine vinegar

vivre: (to) live

voir: (to) see

(la) voiture: (the) car

voler: (to) fly

vouloir: (to) want

vous: you (formal and/or plural pronoun)

voyager: (to) travel

W

(le) wagon: (the) railway carriage, (the) railcar

(le) week-end: (the) weekend

(le) Wi-Fi: (the) Wi-Fi

Y

(le) yacht: (the) yacht

(le) yaourt: (the) yogurt

(le) yaourt aux fruits: (the) yogurt with fruits

(le) yaourt biologique: (the) organic yogurt (biologique can be shortened to bio as well)

(le) yaourt glacé: (the) frozen yogurt

Z

(le) zeste: (the) zest

(le) zeste de citron: (the) lemon zest

(le) zeste d'orange: (the) orange zest

(le) zoo: (the) zoo

Cardinal Numbers: 0 thru 100

zéro: zero // 0

un: one // 1

deux: two // 2

trois: three // 3

quatre: four // 4

cinq: five // 5

six: six // 6

sept: seven // 7

huit: eight // 8

neuf: nine // 9

dix: ten // 10

onze: eleven // 11

douze: twelve // 12

treize: thirteen // 13

quatorze: fourteen // 14

quinze: fifteen // 15

seize: sixteen // 16

dix-sept: seventeen // 17

dix-huit: eighteen // 18

dix-neuf: nineteen // 19

vingt: twenty // 20

vingt-et-un: twenty-one // 21

vingt-deux: twenty-two // 22

vingt-trois: twenty-three // 23

vingt-quatre: twenty-four // 24

vingt-cinq: twenty-five // 25

vingt-six: twenty-six // 26

vingt-sept: twenty-seven // 27

vingt-huit: twenty-eight // 28

vingt-neuf: twenty-nine // 29

trente: thirty // 30

trente-et-un: thirty-one // 31

trente-deux: thirty-two // 32

trente-trois: thirty-three // 33

trente-quatre: thirty-four // 34

trente-cinq: thirty-five // 35

trente-six: thirty-six // 36

trente-sept: thirty-seven // 37

trente-huit: thirty-eight // 38

trente-neuf: thirty-nine // 39

quarante: forty // 40

quarante-et-un: forty-one // 41

quarante-deux: forty-two // 42

quarante-trois: forty-three // 43

quarante-quatre: forty-four // 44

quarante-cinq: forty-five // 45

quarante-six: forty-six // 46

quarante-sept: forty-seven // 47

quarante-huit: forty-eight // 48

quarante-neuf: forty-nine // 49

cinquante: fifty // 50

cinquante-et-un: fifty-one // 51

cinquante-deux: fifty-two // 52

cinquante-trois: fifty-three // 53

cinquante-quatre: fifty-four // 54

cinquante-cinq: fifty-five // 55

cinquante-six: fifty-six // 56

cinquante-sept: fifty-seven // 57

cinquante-huit: fifty-eight // 58

cinquante-neuf: fifty-nine // 59

soixante: sixty // 60

soixante-et-un: sixty-one // 61

soixante-deux: sixty-two // 62

soixante-trois: sixty-three // 63

soixante-quatre: sixty-four // 64

soixante-cinq: sixty-five // 65

soixante-six: sixty-six // 66

soixante-sept: sixty-seven // 67

soixante-huit: sixty-eight // 68

soixante-neuf: sixty-nine // 69

soixante-dix: seventy // 70

soixante-et-onze: seventy-one // 71

soixante-douze: seventy-two // 72

soixante-treize: seventy-three // 73

soixante-quatorze: seventy-four // 74

soixante-quinze: seventy-five // 75

soixante-seize: seventy-six // 76

soixante-dix-sept: seventy-seven // 77

soixante-dix-huit: seventy-eight // 78

soixante-dix-neuf: seventy-nine // 79

quatre-vingts: eighty // 80

quatre-vingt-un: eighty-one // 81

quatre-vingt-deux: eighty-two // 82

quatre-vingt-trois: eighty-three // 83

quatre-vingt-quatre: eighty-four // 84

quatre-vingt-cinq: eighty-five // 85

quatre-vingt-six: eighty-six // 86

quatre-vingt-sept: eighty-seven // 87

quatre-vingt-huit: eighty-eight // 88

quatre-vingt-neuf: eighty-nine // 89

quatre-vingt-dix: ninety // 90

quatre-vingt-onze: ninety-one // 91

quatre-vingt-douze: ninety-two // 92

quatre-vingt-treize: ninety-three // 93

quatre-vingt-quatorze: ninety-four // 94

quatre-vingt-quinze: ninety-five // 95

quatre-vingt-seize: ninety-six // 96

quatre-vingt-dix-sept: ninety-seven // 97

quatre-vingt-dix-huit: ninety-eight // 98

quatre-vingt-dix-neuf: ninety-nine // 99

cent: one hundred // 100

Ordinal Numbers: 1st thru 10th

premier: first (masculine) // 1st

première: first (feminine) // 1st

deuxième: second (masculine) // 2nd

seconde: second (feminine) // 2nd

troisième: third // 3rd

quatrième: fourth // 4th

cinquième: fifth // 5th

sixième: sixth // 6th

septième: seventh // 7th

huitième: eighth // 8th

neuvième: ninth // 9th

dixième: tenth // 10th

Months of the Year

(le) janvier: (the) January

(le) février: (the) February

(le) mars: (the) March

(le) avril: (the) April

(le) mai: (the) May

(le) juin: (the) June

(le) juillet: (the) July

(le) août: (the) August

(le) septembre: (the) September

(le) octobre: (the) October

(le) novembre: (the) November

(le) décembre: (the) December

Days of the Week

(le) jour de la semaine: (the) day of the week

(le) dimanche: (the) Sunday

(le) lundi: (the) Monday

(le) mardi: (the) Tuesday

(le) mercredi: (the) Wednesday

(le) jeudi: (the) Thursday

(le) vendredi: (the) Friday

(le) samedi: (the) Saturday

Seasons

(la) saison: (the) season

(le) printemps: (the) spring

l'été: (the) summer

l'automne: (the) autumn

l'hiver: (the) winter

Nationalities

(la) nationalité: (the) nationality

l'Allemand(e): (the) German person

l'Américain(e): (the) American person

l'Arabe: (the) Arab person (both genders)

l'Arménien(ne): (the) Armenian person

(le) Belge: (the) Belgian person (male)

(la) Belge: (the) Belgian person (female)

(le) Brésilien: (the) Brazilian person (male)

(la) Brésilienne: (the) Brazilian person (female)

(le) Britannique: (the) British person (male)

(la) Britannique: (the) British person (female)

(le) Bulgare: (the) Bulgarian person (male)

(la) Bulgare: (the) Bulgarian person (female)

(le) Canadien: (the) Canadian person (male)

(la) Canadienne: (the) Canadian person (female)

(le) Chinois: (the) Chinese person (male)

(la) Chinoise: (the) Chinese person (female)

(le) Coréen: (the) Korean person (male)

(la) Coréenne: (the) Korean person (female)

l'Espagnol(e): (the) Spanish person

(le) Français: (the) French person (male)

(la) Française: (the) French person (female)

(le) Grec: (the) Greek person (male)

(la) Grecque: (the) Greek person (female)

l'Indien(ne): (the) Indian person

l'Italien(ne): (the) Italian person

(le) Japonais: (the) Japanese person (male)

(la) Japonaise: (the) Japanese person (female)

(le) Marocain: (the) Moroccan person (male)

(la) Marocaine: (the) Moroccan person (female)

(le) Mexicain: (the) Mexican person (male)

(la) Mexicaine: (the) Mexican person (female)

(le) Polonais: (the) Polish person (male)

(la) Polonaise: (the) Polish person (female)

(le) Portugais: (the) Portuguese person (male)

(la) Portugaise: (the) Portuguese person (female)

(le) Roumain: (the) Romanian person (male)

(la) Roumaine: (the) Romanian person (female)

(le) Russe: (the) Russian person (male)

(la) Russe: (the) Russian person (female)

(le) Suisse: (the) Swiss person (male)

(la) Suissesse: (the) Swiss person (female)

(le) Turc: (the) Turkish person (male)

(la) Turque: (the) Turkish person (female)

(le) Vietnamien: (the) Vietnamese person (male)

(la) Vietnamienne: (the) Vietnamese person (female)

Colors

(la) couleur: (the) color

doré(e): gold

argenté(e): silver

rouge: red

orange: orange

jaune: yellow

vert(e): green

bleu(e): blue

violet(te): purple

rose: pink

blanc(he): white

noir(e): black

gris(e): gray

brun(e): brown (describing hair, skin, or fur color)

marron: brown (describing objects)

Acknowledgements

Svyatoslav Albireo is a multifaceted professional with a passion for language, literature, and human connection. As the founder of Albireo MKG (Meine Kreative Gruppe), he collaborates with family members on various creative projects. Albireo's academic background in linguistics and psychology, coupled with his polyglot abilities, informs his work as a translator, foreign language instructor, and writer.

Through his writing, Albireo aims to contribute positively to humanity, adhering to the principle that literature should serve as a catalyst for improving lives. His unique perspective and dedication to his craft make him a valuable voice in contemporary literature. He writes in the genres of science fiction, fairy tales, fantasy, dark fantasy, horror, and social prose.

Join the "World Aficionados" Community!

Would you like to be a part of a private Facebook community organized by Black Swan Languages that seeks to facilitate an accurate understanding of the rest of the world while forging new global friendships?

If yes, click on the link below or scan the QR code on this page with your phone's camera app. Let's make the world better connected, one day at a time!

Join Here: **https://www.facebook.com/share/g/1AdYDsxSZp/**

Scan This QR Code
with Your Camera
to Join!

Resources

1. Bakanov, Alexandr. "Paris skyline France eiffel sketch drawn vector." Depositphotos, depositphotos.com/vector/paris-skyline-france-eiffel-sketch-drawn-vector-80664836.html.

2. Claudia. "The key Vocabulary That You Will Need for the DELF A1 - French Exam." French Exam, 16 July 2013, www.french-exam.com/vocabulary-that-is-needed-for-the-delf-a1.

3. "Curse Casual" font (source: https://www.dafont.com/curse-casual-jve.font) by Jayvee D. Enaguas (Grand Chaos), licensed under Creative Commons Attribution-ShareAlike 3.0 (CC BY-SA 3.0, https://creativecommons.org/licenses/by-sa/3.0/).

4. Davoust, Laurent. "Paris city aerial view from the Buttes-Chaumont, Paris." Depositphotos, depositphotos.com/photo/paris-city-aerial-view-from-the-

buttes-chaumont-paris-335453968.html.

5. Dementieva, Uliana. "French cheese - round camembert with basil leaves on a wooden background." Depositphotos, depositphotos.com/photo/french-cheese-camembert-basil-leaves-wooden-background-262284178.html.

6. Eden. "A1 French Study Guide | A Clear View Of What To Learn." Learn To French, 24 Oct. 2022, learntofrench.com/a1-french-study-guide.

7. Elodie. "Complete guide to the DELF A1 Syllabus." Youronlinefrenchteacher, 27 Feb. 2023, www.youronlinefrenchteacher.com/complete-guide-to-the-delf-a1-syllabus.

8. Emelyanenko, Andrey. "Eiffel Tower at night. France. Paris." Depositphotos, depositphotos.com/photo/eiffel-tower-at-night-france-paris-144155321.html.

9. Gueret, Pascale. "Paris, Luxembourg garden, beautiful flowerbeds in spring." Depositphotos, depositphotos.com/photo/paris-luxembourg-garden-beautiful-flowerbeds-spring-231795058.html.

10. Jarmolowicz, Anastasija. "Eiffel Tower and fountains of Trocadero." Depositphotos, depositphotos.com/photo/eiffel-tower-and-fountains-of-t rocadero-47247825.html.

11. ---. "Facade of Paris opera house, France." Depositphotos, depositphotos.com/photo/facade-of-paris-opera-house-fr ance-22313589.html.

12. Kolesnyk, Sergii. "Tower near park in Paris." Depositphotos, depositphotos.com/photo/tower-near-park-in-paris-1540 55746.html.

13. Language Knowledge / Eu - Explore Language Knowledge in Europe. languageknowledge.eu/countries/france.

14. Matrosova, Larisa. "Open sandwich tartine with tomato, ham, garlic and cheese." Depositphotos, depositphotos.com/photo/open-sandwich-tartine-tomato -ham-garlic-cheese-225194058.html.

15. Mazza, Alberto. "Staircase of Sacred Heart." Depositphotos, depositphotos.com/photo/staircase-of-sacred-heart-2041 91926.html.

16. Miragaya, Karel. "The Louvre Museum in Paris." Depositphotos, depositphotos.com/photo/the-louvre-museum-in-paris-182997644.html.

17. Pimborough, David William. "Croque Monsieur French Cheese and Ham Sandwich." Depositphotos, depositphotos.com/photo/croque-monsieur-french-cheese-and-ham-sandwich-89750400.html.

18. Prokopenko, Oleksandr. "Mille-feuille with fresh cherry." Depositphotos, depositphotos.com/photo/mille-feuille-with-fresh-cherry-90623112.html.

19. Schram, Anneke. "Tarte Tatin in French." Depositphotos, depositphotos.com/photo/tarte-tatin-in-french-10094319.html.

20. Skalovskaia, Elena. "The grand colorful mosque in the city of Paris." Depositphotos, depositphotos.com/photo/grand-colorful-mosque-city-paris-458703544.html.

21. Sunrise and Sunset Times in Paris. www.timeanddate.com/sun/france/paris.

22. Van Urk, Tromp Willem. "City Park Jardin Des Plants With Natural History Museum in Paris." Depositphotos, depositphotos.com/photo/city-park-jardin-des-plants-with-natural-history-museum-in-paris-77668594.html.

23. Wikipedia contributors. "Administrative Divisions of France." Wikipedia, 26 Feb. 2025, en.wikipedia.org/wiki/Administrative_divisions_of_France.

24. ---. "Circles of Latitude Between the 45th Parallel North and the 50th Parallel North." Wikipedia, 2 Apr. 2025, en.wikipedia.org/wiki/Circles_of_latitude_between_the_45th_parallel_north_and_the_50th_parallel_north#48th_parallel_north.

25. ---. "Municipal Arrondissements of France." Wikipedia, 20 Feb. 2025, en.wikipedia.org/wiki/Municipal_arrondissements_of_France.

26. Wodicka, Erwin. "Paris, france. place du tertre." Depositphotos, depositphotos.com/photo/paris-france-place-de-tertre-10963411.html.